This book, What D[...] in Australia who ha[...] people know what th[...] believe about the Scriptures? From there, God brought other Christians together from various parts of the United States to write what you now hold in your hands. Each one of the authors and editors who were involved with this project know the huge amount of prayer, sacrifice, and hard work that went into making sure we stayed the course, making sure everything lined up with God's Word. I have no doubt in my mind that many people, both Amish and non-Amish, will read What Do the Amish Believe and walk away forever changed.

Joe Keim
Director of MAP Ministry

A book of this nature is long overdue, as I seriously doubt that many Amish lay-people could articulate what they believe and why they believe it. My hope is that many who are serious about their Amish beliefs will compare them with the Scriptures and some of the early Anabaptist writings listed in this book. It is frightfully easy to become immersed in word-of-mouth, cultural, and doctrinal beliefs which may or may not line up with the Scriptures. This book should give people a Scriptural basis for their beliefs.

Hank Hershberger
Translator of the Pennsylvania Dutch Bible

The information in *What Do the Amish Believe?* is laid out in a way that is very easy to understand. I think the book will help others understand what the Amish believe. Also, the writers did an amazing job!

Rose Edna Burkholder

First of all, I really have a lot of respect and appreciation for this book and its authors. It does a very good job explaining where the Amish come from and why they are where they are today. It explains well what a Christian's relationship with Jesus Christ should look like. It was interesting in the second chapter to read that knowing God does not save you. Even Satan knows God but trembles. Rather, you must put your faith in Jesus Christ and serve him. Chapter three does a fantastic job of explaining the Trinity and especially the Holy Spirit. I grew up not knowing or hearing much about the Holy Spirit, but this book thoroughly explains the importance of the presence of the Holy Spirit in Christians. This is a very good book for everyone to read.

Jeptha & Fannie Yoder

Just as it would be difficult to try to narrow down one specific list of Baptist or Presbyterian beliefs that fits every Baptist or Presbyterian group and individual, so it is not an easy task to compile a book of Amish beliefs that fits every Amish community and individual. There will, of course, be variations among groups, but this book is a great place to begin. Starting with one of the earliest Anabaptist confessions of faith, learn what the early Anabaptists wrote down and agreed upon. Then continue reading as the Bible is discussed.

This would be good for Anabaptists to read to review what their ancestors wrote and consider again what the Bible says, that this book might encourage them to continue reading and following the Bible – the Holy Book for which so many Anabaptists gave their lives. This book would also be good for others who are interested in learning the basics of what the Amish and Mennonites believe and would be a good starting point to discuss biblical topics with their Anabaptist neighbors and friends. May this book, What Do the Amish Believe?, encourage all to study the Word of God more fully, to know what they believe, and to live lives according to the Holy Scriptures.

Paul E. Miller
Ashland, Ohio

WHAT DO THE
Amish
BELIEVE?

WHAT DO THE
Amish
BELIEVE?

**The Doctrine of the Plain People
Compared with Scripture**

Compiled by Aneko Press
and MAP Ministry

Visit the MAP Ministry website:
www.mapministry.org

Printed in the United States of America
Aneko Press – *Our Readers Matter*[TM]
www.anekopress.com
Aneko Press, Life Sentence Publishing, and our logos are trademarks of
Life Sentence Publishing, Inc.
203 E. Birch Street
P.O. Box 652
Abbotsford, WI 54405
RELIGION / Christianity / Amish
Paperback ISBN: 978-1-62245-404-4
eBook ISBN: 978-1-62245-405-1
10 9 8 7 6 5 4 3 2 1
Available from MAP Ministry and wherever books are sold.

Contents

Many thanks to the people who have helped bring this project to fruition: Lester Graber, Jim Elder, Joe Keim, Paul Miller, Steve Mishler, Geoff Smith, Charlotte Wagner, Benjamin Szumskyj, and John Bouquet. We appreciate the research, writing talents, and love you put into this project.

FOREWORD

Jeremiah Zeiset

I was raised Old Order Mennonite, and the Plain People
(Amish and Mennonites) have a special place in my heart.
While the church I came from wasn't Amish, our beliefs were
much the same – probably more similar in many ways than to
our less conservative Mennonite church brethren. We shared
our one-room schools with the Amish, our heart language was
Pennsylvania Dutch, and we strove with nearly the same tenacity
to stay separate from the world in the way we looked and lived.

When I was in my upper teens, a coworker asked me about my
faith in Christ. I said, "Yes, I believe in Jesus Christ." When he
asked me if I knew where I was going when I died, I responded
as many other Plain People would – that I had a hope of going
to heaven, but I wouldn't know for sure until I appeared before
the judgment seat. My coworker was confident he would go to
heaven, because the Bible said he would if he placed his faith in
Christ. I, on the other hand, was just as confident that I could
only "hope" to go to heaven.

While I couldn't dare to say I was sure of my eternal destina-
tion, the reality was that I couldn't refer to Bible verses to back

up my belief. Furthermore, I was quite uncomfortable talking about my faith, partly because I wasn't used to conversations like that and simply didn't know very much about the Bible, God, or any other spiritual topic. In fact, I really didn't like people who talked about God a lot and who seemed overly "spiritual."

Since that conversation, I've had plenty of time to ponder just what it was I believed. The more I considered it, the less I knew for sure what I believed. I think the same is true for others, too; too many, unfortunately, don't know exactly what they believe. Few have a comprehensive understanding of Scripture, and few know for sure what will happen when they die. It's even more unfortunate when preachers and parents discourage congregations and children from spending "too much" time studying the Bible.

Friend, our forefathers didn't perish for a lack of knowledge (Hosea 4:6). Ulrich Zwingli, one of the central figures in the Anabaptist movement, was noted for starting a Bible study with a group of eager young men. These people left everything in a desperate pursuit of the true God of the Bible. The prominent church of the time promoted extra-biblical teachings, and it didn't sit well with these heroes of faith. Is anything less expected of us? We must pursue God with the same relentlessness, desiring to know Him personally, loving the things He loves, and rejecting anything added to or subtracted from God's Word.

This book was originally the idea of an Australian man named Benjamin Szumskyj. He has a sincere love for the Plain People and said he could find no books that defined Plain theology, one of the only religions in the world of which this is true. Our initial goal was to publish this book for non-Plain people who were interested in knowing what the Plain People believed. However, as we worked on the project, we realized that there are Amish and Mennonites like me, people who have questions concerning exactly what it is that they believe, people who would also want to read this book.

The purpose of this book is to define just what it is that Amish and Old Order Mennonites believe today; this is a book for both the Plain and the non-Plain. We cover topics such as Who Is God? What Is the Church? What Happens at the End? and more. There are many different Amish groups, and while not all groups believe the same, the writers of this book relied heavily on Anabaptist writings such as the *Dordrecht Confession of Faith,* and also spoke with other Anabaptists to make sure they were accurately portraying what the majority of Plain People believe.

We follow up each topic with what the Bible says on the subject. This allows you to compare and contrast what is commonly believed by the Plain People with what the Bible teaches. We also strongly suggest you spend time to be sure of what you believe. Why is this so important? Because our salvation is not dependent on a set of rules or on our church's teachings, but on a *personal* relationship with Christ. Your salvation depends on your belief on the Lord Jesus Christ (salvation by faith, Acts 16:31) as much as your reward in heaven depends on your own righteous works according to the abilities you are given (Matthew 25:14-30). You may already know this, but as you peel back the layers even further, you will find deeper meaning and fulfillment in your walk with the Lord. If you're like I was, you may even find that you know *about* the Lord, but don't yet know Him personally. If that's the way you feel, know that you're not the first person to come to this realization, and also know that there is an understandable way to know Him for yourself.

Also, while this book will be helpful, be sure to pray and ask the Lord to reveal truth to you. I know from personal experience that we must be open to the truth and that the Holy Spirit is the one who reveals truths to us – no book or preacher can do this, but only the Holy Spirit. *But the Comforter, which is the Holy Ghost, whom the Father will send in my name, he shall teach you all things, and bring all things to your remembrance, whatsoever I have said unto you* (John 14:26). I've personally found that as I ask the Lord to reveal truth to me, He does. And the more I allow Him to show me, the more freedom I find in Jesus Christ, and the more I look forward to spending time reading the Bible and praying. I now look forward to meeting Jesus Christ in the hereafter, knowing that I am secure in His righteousness and that God will look on Jesus Christ and not on me, because my faith is in Him.

Read this book and then be like the Bereans in Acts 17:11:

> *These were more noble than those in Thessalonica, in that **they received the word with all readiness of mind, and searched the scriptures daily,** whether those things were so.*

HISTORY OF THE OLD ORDERS

Dr. Ken Rathbun

In the sixteenth century, during the European Reformation, many people held religious beliefs that didn't fit into the Catholic or Reformer molds. Several religious leaders emerged in Zurich, Switzerland, and nearby areas in the 1520s, where they won converts to their point of view. Scholars and historians often give various labels to these groups. However, in that important decade, names and labels which are familiar to us now were not clearly defined. *Anabaptist* was one such label.

People often refer to any and every group that wasn't Catholic or Protestant during the Reformation as Anabaptist, whether or not that group believed the views common to true Anabaptists. Because this book looks at what the Amish believe, it offers a brief sketch of the history of the Anabaptists who later called themselves Mennonites. This brief overview will focus primarily on their beginnings.

Reformer Ulrich Zwingli

In January 1525, a momentous event took place in Zurich. The Reformer Ulrich Zwingli had worked for several years to overthrow the Catholic Church and replace it with his own vision of a state-enforced reformation movement. He criticized papal authority and warned people of the uselessness of earning their way to heaven through the honoring of relics, religious processions, and visiting holy sites. He taught that salvation came through faith in Christ alone.

Eager young men flocked around Zwingli to study the Bible and theology. They believed in justification (to be made right or declared innocent) by faith alone for their salvation. As they learned Bible study methods from their teacher, these men began to question the widespread tradition of baptizing babies. Eventually, this concern caused divisions within the town. With Zwingli's encouragement, the city council voted in mid-January 1525 to require infant baptism of all births. He thought it was important that a person be "born" into the state church and that God's church should include all the people in a given area. However, he also believed that the church is born of the Word of God, and that Christ alone is its head. In direct opposition to this command to baptize babies, the men of Zwingli's Bible study met one evening to baptize each other as believers. This new group became known as *Anabaptists,* which meant *rebaptizers.*

Of those who participated in that historic night (January 21, 1525), all suffered persecution, exile, and slander for their belief. Some were killed. That first Anabaptist baptism took place in the home of Felix Manz. George Blaurock, Conrad Grebel, and others also participated. Manz was later drowned for his faith in Zurich (a cruel irony for those who professed believer's baptism in water). Blaurock was beaten in Zurich, then exiled, and eventually burned at the stake in Austria. Grebel died of the plague after a brief preaching ministry.

The questioning of infant baptism as a means of salvation came from the reading and study of Scripture. This new group's findings gave them the courage to act upon their beliefs and to go against both the religious and civil authorities. Other people in the region also found the biblical arguments for believer's baptism logical and convincing.

The topic of baptism was an issue within a wider area of disagreement – namely one's view of the church. The Reformers had a different understanding of the church than these Anabaptists. The Anabaptists believed a church should be free from the control of the government, and church membership should be voluntary, not based on the baptism of an innocent infant. They were also against persecuting people for their beliefs. While these ideas might not seem earth-shattering to us today, in the sixteenth century, many who accepted these views suffered horribly.

Other Reformers

Michael Sattler also contributed to the founding of Anabaptism. He was highly regarded by several Reformers in Strasbourg, even though he was exiled from Zurich for his Anabaptist beliefs. In February 1527, he authored the first statement of distinctives (differences) in Switzerland called the Schleitheim Brotherly Union. Many Anabaptists adopted this confession, more commonly known as the Schleitheim Confession. It promoted believer's baptism, church discipline practiced by the local church, a memorial view of the Lord's Supper, holy living for church members, qualifications of pastors, non-resistance (no participation in the military), and the prohibition (forbidding) of making oaths. In May of that year, Sattler was caught, tried, tortured, and burned for his faith.

Another champion of baptism based on a prior salvation decision was Balthazar Hubmaier. This highly-educated former priest wrote several influential books against infant baptism and persecution for one's beliefs. His arguments were difficult for the Reformers to answer, and he is well known for how he ended his books with the classic phrase "Truth is immortal." He was tortured in Zurich and later burned at the stake in Austria in 1528. The loss of such stable leadership directly affected later events.

Other beliefs and ideas regarding how to go about reform and break from the Catholic Church came from non-Protestants during the 1520s and later. If any idea united these groups (and it is difficult to find one), it was the idea of a church separate from the control of the state. Crucial to all non-Catholic and non-Protestant groups was what they viewed as their ultimate or final authority. The Anabaptists described above highly valued the New Testament. Other groups preferred the Old Testament. Additional groups, known as Spiritualists, valued the Bible, yet placed a greater emphasis on revelation received from God.

Religious leaders in that day often gathered followers by their forceful preaching. More than a few leaders "received" prophetic messages predicting a final battle and the coming of Christ. Strasbourg (then in Germany) and later, Münster, were each identified at one time or another by one of these leaders as the New Jerusalem. In 1534, one of these groups forcefully seized control of Münster and proclaimed it the capital of Christ's kingdom. After much violence within the city, a combined Lutheran and Catholic army retook the city and brutally executed the leaders.

Though Anabaptism would long be remembered and harshly criticized for the events at Münster, it remains a fact of history that Anabaptists made non-resistance and non-participation in the military one of their distinctive key characteristics. (Mennonites and Amish today are one of the largest Christian non-resistance groups in the world.)

Menno Simons

During this same time in northern Holland, a Catholic priest with an uneasy conscience gained fame by preaching against obvious Catholic abuses. After learning about Anabaptism and studying Scripture, he became convinced infant baptism was wrong. However, he struggled with separating from his church and joining the now-discredited Anabaptists. After seeing many of them (including his own family members) suffer, he took compassion on these scattered, leaderless groups. He knew the way forward would be treacherous, lonely, and difficult, but in 1536 he gave up his secure position and joined the Anabaptists. His name was Menno Simons.

Menno lived a life filled with constant travail and harassment, including hiding from and escaping from religious authorities. Amid these hardships, he provided essential leadership which held the Dutch and North German Anabaptists together. His writings showed a desire to help his extended flock and a concern for church discipline. The impact of his ministry is demonstrated by the fact that eventually many Anabaptist groups in locations far from Menno's area of ministry were called Mennonites. However, Menno held an unusual view of the origin of Christ's flesh, and it was a view that his later followers did not hold.

Anabaptism grew in strength in Holland, North and South Germany, Switzerland, and Moravia. The only effective way of limiting its impact was persecution. The Catholics, especially, killed many, as the *Martyrs Mirror* recounts. The Reformers' common method of exiling Anabaptists from their regions frequently resulted in the death of the exiled one, as the Catholics often burned the Anabaptists fleeing the Reformers' territories. Because of this hardship, some Anabaptists even tried communalism (all possessions were owned by the community). Anabaptism continued in Switzerland, but persecution continued.

Some Anabaptists relocated north to the Rhine River Valley, where they enjoyed greater freedom for a time.

Jakob Ammann

In 1693, a division arose among the Swiss Anabaptists that is still apparent today. An elder named Jakob Ammann expressed dissatisfaction with the way the brethren lived out their faith. Ammann wanted to see stricter separation from the world in rigorous disciples of Christ, as well as church discipline with the practice of shunning, even for family members. He also expected obedience to the *1632 Dordrecht Confession of Faith*, which included foot washing as an ordinance of the church, which the Swiss congregations had not observed.

The conflict raged not only in Switzerland, but also in the Rhine Valley, including southern Germany and Alsace (located in France). After much discussion, the conflict remained unresolved, and the stricter Anabaptists took the name of their leader and became known as the Amish.

Persecution during this time by governmental authorities never ceased. With news of available land in the New World and other places, immigration seemed to offer relief from oppression, and the thought of relocating interested many Anabaptist groups. In some regions, immigration was actually forced upon them by the rulers.

Relocation

While moving to a new world offered freedom to follow their beliefs, relocation also brought challenges of how to preserve their identity in new settings. Concerns about religious beliefs, culture, appearance, and language were important to both

Mennonites and Amish. To what extent these issues caused problems differed among the various groups.

Beginning in the eighteenth century, many Mennonite and Amish groups travelled to North America to start a new life. They often settled in Pennsylvania, though movement westward was ongoing as farmlands grew scarce. Some settled in Ontario as well. Later, both the midwestern United States and the western provinces of Canada saw many settlements of those from the Anabaptist heritage.

Beginning in the 1760s, some Mennonite groups in Germany and Switzerland travelled east into Russia. They enjoyed a long and often profitable existence, until the rise of communism in the 1920s. When that happened, many tried to leave for North and South America.

The stricter Mennonite and Amish faced a number of challenges when relocating. One of the challenges dealt with the extent to which they were to apply the principles of strict discipleship to Christ. These groups saw conformity to the world as directly opposed to faithfulness to Christ. Standards of how this loyalty to Christ proved itself in response to technology and industry caused conflict over time. They prized simplicity, separation from worldliness, and the daily practice of their faith. Specific rules demonstrating these concerns were classified in their *Ordnung*, an unwritten set of guidelines for life and conduct. Over time, however, not all agreed on the everyday application of these principles.

In the 1870s, the Amish in the United States became divided, and the stricter among them formed the Old Order Amish. The remaining, progressive-minded Amish joined together as Amish Mennonites. In the early twentieth century, more and more groups united, and the Amish Mennonites became known simply as Mennonites. Some joined the Mennonite Conference churches. Today, the Old Order Amish maintain their distinctions with practices including social shunning, foot washing, strictness in dress and appearance, and shunning of technology. The Old Order Mennonites formed during the late nineteenth century, and they, too, favored traditional forms of living and limited use of technology.

Immigration didn't always mean freedom in every sense for the Amish or Mennonites. Though they enjoyed church membership based on the baptism of believers, the liberty to practice their beliefs raised other issues which proved difficult. Neighbors and local authorities of these German-speaking arrivals did not always accept them, and at the national level, the United States government did not always embrace the non-resistance of these pacifist churches. This difficulty continued at least through World War I. The laws regarding the education of their children were also trying, especially in the twentieth century for those in the United States and Canada.

In Europe throughout the latter nineteenth century, the Amish trend of merging with the Mennonites was apparent. In 1937, the last Amish church united with a Mennonite congregation.

In the twentieth century, the Old Order Amish and Mennonites in North America faced the challenge of disunity within their ranks. Groups formed that favored greater use of technology and less strictness in their personal lives. Despite these conflicts, the Old Order Amish experienced a strong growth rate (which continues today), and the retention rate of children deciding to receive baptism and remain in the Old Order are extremely high.

The future of the Old Order Amish and Mennonites will be determined on one hand by whether or not they maintain their distinct plain appearance and customs. More important, however, will be whether or not each generation will first and foremost seek salvation by faith and maintain a clean heart for the Lord.

Chapter 1

<u>GOD</u>

Theology

For though there be that are called gods, whether in heaven or in earth, (as there be gods many, and lords many,) but to us there is but one God, the Father, of whom are all things. (1 Corinthians 8:5-6)

I am the LORD and there is none else, there is no God beside me. (Isaiah 45:5)

I am the LORD: that is my name: and my glory will I not give to another, neither my praise to graven images. (Isaiah 42:8)

Introduction

Have you ever tried to describe God to someone? God is so far beyond description that our human language seems inadequate to give a proper portrayal of Him. Yet He has given us a Book in which He describes Himself in a way that we can comprehend and come to know Him, the High and Holy God.

Some see God as the Almighty Judge – harsh, almost slow to forgive, and quick to administer punishment to all who disobey the rules. Others see Him as the all-inclusive God of love – tenderhearted, slow to anger, and quick to forgive. Is it possible that both these characteristics are true?

We often form our viewpoint of God from those who preach the Word of God to us. Even though they mean well and their motive is right, they tend to portray God according to their own thoughts. The blending of God's judgment and grace is an age-old battle in Christendom. Those who dwell on God's holiness vs. man's sinfulness will focus on man's behavior – continually judging and warning people of God's certain punishment. On the other hand, those who dwell on God's love and forgiveness will claim that God could never condemn anyone to an eternal punishment – focusing on man's efforts in spite of his continued falling into sin. Both views are misleading. Those who hold to only one side have swerved away from the center of God's teachings, because they have failed to thoroughly study God's Word with a teachable heart. If we work to balance judgment and love, and carefully and consistently study the Scriptures, we are able to come to a right understanding of who God is, and realize that He makes it possible for us to know Him in a very personal way.

What the Amish Teach

The *Dordrecht Confession of Faith* does not have a specific section on who God is, but it does give us an idea of what the original Anabaptists believed about God.

Article 1

God is "a rewarder of them that seek Him . . . eternal, almighty, and incomprehensible God, the Father, Son, and Holy Ghost" (Hebrews 11:6; Genesis 17:1; 1 John 5:7). He is the only God, "before whom no God was made or existed nor shall exist after Him: for from Him, through

Him, and in Him, are all things." He is eternal, receiving "praise and honor forever and ever" (Romans 11:36). He is a creative and powerful God. He "created, made, and prepared, heaven and earth, and the sea and all that in them is" (Acts 14:15). He is all knowing. "He still governs and upholds the same [the universe] . . . through His wisdom, might, and the word of His power." He created all things "good and upright, according to His pleasure," thus, He is righteous and holy (Genesis 1-2).

Article 2

As a holy God, He does not tolerate sin, but judges man for his sin. Man's disobedience "brought upon themselves the wrath of God, and condemnation" (Romans 5:12, 18).

Article 3

God is loving and kind. God was "not willing to cast them off entirely, or to let them be forever lost. . . ." He provided a means of restoration and reconciliation (making peace) for the human race. He is a merciful and gracious God (1 Peter 1:19-20; 1 John 2:1).

Article 4

God is faithful; He kept his promise for the coming Messiah (John 4:25).

Article 10

God wants to have "unity and fellowship" with mankind. He is a personable God (Acts 2:42, 46).

Article 18

God is a living God – the giver of life; He will raise up

the dead at the last day. God is a judgmental God; He will judge the works of man in the last day (Matthew 22:30-32; John 5:28; 2 Corinthians 5:10; 1 Corinthians 15; Revelation 20:12).

The Apostles' Creed also attests to the belief in an all-powerful Creator God who is the Trinity, the eternal Judge, and forgiving God.

A more detailed description of God is found in the Second Confession of Faith, drawn up in Amsterdam in 1630 and published in the *Martyrs Mirror*. It states:

> We believe with the heart, and confess with the mouth, that there is one only, eternal, incomprehensible [hard to understand], spiritual Being, which, in Scripture, is called God; to whom alone is ascribed [credited] omnipotence [all-powerful], mercy, righteousness, perfection, wisdom, all goodness, and omniscience [all-knowing], and who is called a fountain of life, and the source of all good, the Creator of all things; and the Preserver of the same; who in the Old Testament bears various appellations [titles] – the God of Abraham, Isaac and Jacob, the God Schadai [Shaddai], the God Jehovah, the God of Israel, I am that I am, the Alpha and Omega, etc.; but who in the New Testament is called by three distinct names – God the Father, Son, and Holy Ghost, whom we confess to differ thus far, namely, that the Father, as far as He is Father, is another than the Son; and the Son, as far as He is Son, is another than the Father, and the Holy Ghost, as far as He is a true Holy Ghost, is another than the Father and the Son, and that they, although differing in name, are nevertheless in their divine nature and attributes, one only, undivided God, according to the testimony of the apostle: *For there are three that bear record in heaven, the*

Father, the Word, and the Holy Ghost: and these three are one (1 John 5:7).

What the Scriptures Teach

Many people say they worship God – Mormons, Baptists, Jehovah's Witnesses, Pentecostals, Amish, Mennonites, Muslims, Catholics, Native Americans, etc. – but do they all worship the same God? Since we have chosen to believe that the God of the Holy Bible is the one true God, we need to know how to answer this question. Many religious people base their knowledge of God only on their own imagination of what they think God should be. Let's take a look at how God describes Himself in the Scriptures, much of which will overlap with what was already discussed about what the Amish believe, but it will be expanded and will further clarify who God is.

Our first introduction to God is Genesis 1:1, which says, *In the beginning God.* In the original Hebrew language, the word for God is *Elohim,* which can be a general term for things or beings that are worshiped. In Genesis 2:4, God introduces Himself as *LORD God.* The English word "LORD," in all capital letters, is the translation of the Hebrew word *Yahweh,* also translated as *Jehovah.* Jehovah was the only God that existed in Genesis 1:1, and He is the only God existing today.

The word *Elohim* is plural, meaning more than one. If God is the *only* God, then why would He use a plural word for Himself as He did in Genesis 1:26? *Let **us** make man in **our** image, after **our** likeness.* As we read the Bible, we see that God is three persons in one God – a Trinity made up of God the Father, God the Son (Jesus Christ), and God the Holy Spirit. They are usually mentioned separately throughout the Old Testament, but are often mentioned together in the New Testament, as in Matthew 28:19: *Go ye therefore, and teach all nations, baptizing* *them in the name of the Father, and of the Son, and of the Holy Ghost.* They are equal in their attributes (qualities), but different in their functions (what they do). For example, God the Father created the universe by His will (Genesis 1), through His Son (John 1:3), and by the power of His Spirit (Genesis 1:2). We do not need to understand it to believe it. God does not lie (Titus 1:2).

Because God is so great and mighty, we find it difficult to describe Him in only a few words. In the Old Testament, however, as the Jewish people had needs, God provided for those needs and then introduced Himself by the name that expressed His quality that was shown in that provision. In this way, the people came to know God. As we learn His names, we can know Him, too. He helped us by describing Himself in this way throughout the Scriptures. Although most of the names of God are translated into English, we will also look at the Hebrew names, remembering that the Hebrew word *El* is the singular form of *Elohim*, meaning "God the Father."

In Genesis 21:33, Abraham *called there on the name of the LORD, the **everlasting God.*** The Hebrew word is *El-Olam*, meaning *Jehovah God is eternal.* The same word is used in Psalm 90:2 where we read: *Before the mountains were brought forth, or ever thou hadst formed the earth and the world, even from everlasting to everlasting, thou art God.* He has no beginning, nor will He have an end.

In Exodus, when God was sending Moses to Pharaoh to bring His people out of Egypt, Moses wanted to know who he should say sent him. God told Moses: ***I AM THAT I AM:*** *Thus shalt thou say unto the children of Israel. I AM hath sent me unto you* (Exodus 3:14). This name of God comes from the Hebrew word *hayah*, which means "exists." In the statement to Moses, He is saying He wants to be known as the "God who is the one God." The Egyptians had many gods, so God was telling them that He was the only God. God does not need anyone or anything to exist, and He is independent of anyone else's power and knowledge.

In Romans 11:33-34 we read: *O the depth of the riches both of the wisdom and knowledge of God! How unsearchable are his judgments, and his ways past finding out! For who hath known the mind of the Lord? Or who hath been his counsellor?* God is *omniscient,* which means He is all-knowing. All knowledge, whether ancient or modern, comes from God, and it is man who uses it for either good or evil. David understood the extent of God's knowledge when he said:

> *O LORD, thou hast searched me, and known me.*
> *Thou knowest my downsitting and mine uprising,*
> *thou understandest my thought afar off.*
>
> *Thou compassest* [takes care of] *my path and my*
> *lying down, and art acquainted with all my ways.*
> *For there is not a word in my tongue, but, lo, O*
> *LORD, thou knowest it altogether. Thou hast beset*
> *me behind and before, and laid thine hand upon me.*
>
> *Such knowledge is too wonderful for me; it is high, I*
> *cannot attain unto it* (Psalm 139:1-6).

As Abram returned from the battle of the kings in Genesis 14, Melchizedek, a priest of *the **most high God,*** came out to meet him, *and he blessed him, and said, Blessed be Abram of the most high God, possessor of heaven and earth: and blessed be the most high God, which hath delivered thine enemies into thy hand* (Genesis 14:19-20). Abram had gone out with only 318 of his servants and defeated the kings who had taken Lot captive. This name of God, the *most high God*, comes from the Hebrew, *Elyon.* It pictures God as king over all. He rules the earth and the universe from heaven. He is sovereign, the highest authority, and the supreme ruler. God has every right to rule over us and tell us how to live and act, for He created us.

And when Abram was ninety years old and nine, the LORD appeared to Abram, and said unto him, I am the **Almighty God***; walk before me, and be thou perfect* (Genesis 17:1). The Hebrew name, *El-Shaddai*, is translated as the all-sufficient, the all-powerful, the all-mighty God. God appeared to Abram to make a covenant with him, and He promised to make him a father of many nations. Considering his age, Abram knew this feat would take God Almighty to accomplish it. Later, *God spake unto Moses, and said unto him, I am the LORD: and I appeared unto Abraham, unto Isaac, and unto Jacob, by the name of* **God Almighty***, but by my name JEHOVAH was I not known to them* (Exodus 6:3).

Name by name, God was making Himself known to the Israelites. The writer of Psalm 91 said, *He that dwelleth in the secret place of the most High shall abide under the shadow of the* **Almighty** (Psalm 91:1). No one, not even Satan, is more powerful than God. He created the universe out of nothing, simply by His spoken word. He is omnipotent – all-powerful and all-mighty. Many of us strive to live as self-sufficiently as we can because we know others will fail us, but we were not made to live independently. We were created to depend on *El-Shaddai* for all our needs.

Ezekiel described the city of Jerusalem at the end of his book. He told where the tribes were to be located, where the borders were, and where the suburbs were. He gave measurements of each side and labeled the gates by the tribes. In the end, he said it *was round about eighteen thousand measures: and the name of the city from that day shall be,* **the LORD is there,** or *Jehovah-shamah* (Ezekiel 48:35). He is omnipresent – in all places at the same time. Psalm 139:7 says, *Whither shall I go from thy spirit? Or whither shall I flee from thy presence?*

And, Jeremiah 23:24 says, *Can any hide himself in secret places that I shall not see him? saith the LORD. Do not I fill heaven and earth?* We are never alone. There is no place that we can go without God being there.

Neither are we ever out of range of God's seeing eye. In Genesis when Hagar fled from Sarai, she hid by a fountain in the wilderness, but God found her. Even in her distress, Hagar *called the name of the LORD that spake unto her,* **Thou God seest me**: *for she said, Have I also here looked after him that seeth me?* (Genesis 16:13). This God who sees is *El-Roi*, a name that is given to help us understand that He sees everything. This fact can be either comforting or daunting, depending on our relationship with Him.

Malachi 3:6 gives us another characteristic that can comfort us. It says, *I am the* **LORD, *I change not.*** Another word for this is *immutable.* If God the Father never changes, neither does His Son nor His Spirit. Hebrews 13:8 tells us *Jesus Christ the same yesterday, and to day, and for ever.* Thus, the God of the Old Testament is the same God as the God of the New Testament. His law still remains the standard of His perfection, but God has now entered into a New Covenant with us through His Son. *But now hath he obtained a more excellent ministry, by how much also he is the mediator of a better covenant, which was established upon better promises* (Hebrews 8:6).

Yes, God *does* change His mind at times, depending on our response to Him. For example, He said that the people of Nineveh had forty days until their destruction. Then, because they repented, He changed His mind. *And Jonah began to enter into the city a day's journey, and he cried, and said, Yet forty days, and Nineveh shall be overthrown. So the people of Nineveh believed God, and proclaimed a fast, and put on sackcloth, from the greatest of them even to the least of them. . . . And God saw their works, that they turned from their evil way; and God repented of the evil, that he had said that he would do unto them; and he did it not* (Jonah 3:4-5, 10). God sometimes may change His mind, but His character, the way He is, never changes.

Behold, the days come, saith the LORD, that I will raise unto David a righteous Branch, and a King shall reign and prosper, and shall execute judgment and justice in the earth. In his days Judah shall be saved, and Israel shall dwell safely: and this is his name whereby he shall be called, **THE LORD OUR RIGHTEOUSNESS** (Jeremiah 23:5-6). This is *Jehovah Tsidkenu.* At the time of this prophecy, the kingdom of Judah was about to fall because of their idolatry, oppression, and violence. This name means that God will always do what is right. Psalm 48:10 says, *According to thy name, O God, so is thy praise unto the ends of the earth: thy right hand is full of righteousness.* He is right all the time. He is never wrong. His holiness demands perfection from His creation. When His created ones disobeyed His one command, His holiness could not tolerate their error. To tolerate sin, any sin, and not separate it from Himself would only stain His holiness. Because of His righteousness, God had to judge Israel and Judah. We would not be loving parents if we allowed our children to cheat, lie, and steal, because we would only be training them to live lives of sin. Likewise, it is God's love and righteousness that made Him judge and punish sin.

When David went to fight Goliath, he was much smaller than Goliath and wore no armor. Goliath made fun of David. *Then said David to the Philistine, Thou comest to me with a sword, and with a spear, and with a shield: but I come to thee in the name of the* **LORD of hosts,** *the God of the armies of Israel, whom thou hast defied* (1 Samuel 17:45). David trusted in the armies of God. This LORD of hosts was *Jehovah-Sabaoth.*

Who is the King of glory? The **LORD of hosts,** *he is the King of glory* (Psalm 24:10). David was a warrior king, and he depended on the LORD of hosts to fight for him and protect him.

But even with all this, if this was all that we knew of God, we would be a people most miserable. Many people have spent their whole lives trying to please God with their sacrificial living in order to gain His favor. These people have failed to notice that Jeremiah 23:6 says, *The LORD is **Our Righteousness**.*

Why would we need His righteousness? Aren't we acceptable people in spite of our sin and as long as we regularly ask forgiveness for our sins? Paul quoted the Old Testament in his letter to the Romans. He said, *There is none righteous, no, not one* (Romans 3:10). All of us are condemned to eternal punishment unless we are clothed in God's righteousness, like Abraham. *Abraham believed God, and it was counted unto him for righteousness. . . . His faith is counted for righteousness* (Romans 4:3, 5). God chooses to make us right with Him by faith in His Son, even though there is nothing in us to offer to God (Romans 3:22). We must be rightly clothed to come into His presence. *I will greatly rejoice in the LORD, my soul shall be joyful in my God; for he hath clothed me with the garments of salvation, he hath covered me with the robe of righteousness* (Isaiah 61:10).

Exodus 17:15 tells us that *Moses built an altar, and called the name of it Jehovah-nissi.* This means the **LORD is my banner**, or the **LORD is conqueror**. He is a God of war. He goes to battle against our enemies and against sin, Satan, and eternal death. Through God the Son, this victory was won at the cross. First Corinthians 15:57 says: *But thanks be to God, which giveth us the victory through our Lord Jesus Christ.* Christ has set us free from the power of sin, the control of Satan, and eternal punishment in hell, and He will continue to defend us to the end. He is our Banner, our Conqueror.

In Exodus, Moses told the people that if they would *hearken to the voice of the LORD thy God* and do all that He commanded them, He would keep the Egyptian diseases from them, because *I am the LORD that healeth thee* (Exodus 15:26). He was *Jehovah-Rapha*. Just as God chose to heal the Israelites from their snakebites by faith, He has chosen to heal our hearts from Satan's bite by faith in His Son, Jesus Christ. John tells us that *as Moses lifted up the serpent in the wilderness, even so must the Son of man be lifted up: That whosoever believeth in him should not perish, but have eternal life* (John 3:14-15). *Jehovah-Rapha* is not only the God *who forgiveth all thine iniquities; who healeth all thy diseases,* but He also *healeth the broken in heart, and bindeth up their wounds* (Psalm 103:3; 147:3).

In Genesis 22, we find the account of the time God told Abraham to offer up his son Isaac. They traveled to Mt. Moriah, and at the time when he was about to slay his son, God stopped him. Then Abraham saw a ram in the brush, and he offered it to God. *And Abraham called the name of that place Jehovah-jireh: as it is said to this day, In the mount of the LORD it shall be seen* (Genesis 22:14). This name is translated *The Lord Who Will See To It.* In other words, He will see when we have a need and provide for us, so the name has come to mean **the LORD will provide.** God provided water, manna, and quail for the Israelites in the desert. He provided bread and meat for Elijah when he was hiding, and Jesus provided wine at the wedding and bread and fish for the multitude. But the loving Judge knew that mankind could never meet His standard of perfection which would enable him to renew a relationship with his Creator. Instead, He provided not only His own righteousness in place of man's, but also His own good works to be done through man by God the Spirit. *For by grace are ye saved through faith; and that not of yourselves: it is the gift of God: Not of works, lest any man should boast. For we are his workmanship, created in Christ Jesus unto good works, which God hath before ordained that we should walk in them* (Ephesians 2:8-10).

One of the greatest qualities of God is that He is love. *He that loveth not knoweth not God; for* **God is love**. . . . *Herein is love, not that we loved God, but that he loved us, and sent his Son to be the propitiation* [payment] *for our sins* (1 John 4:8, 10). Jeremiah tells us that God said, *I have loved thee with an everlasting love* (Jeremiah 31:3). How could anything be better than that?

Within the first three commandments of Exodus 20, God declared that He is the only true God, and we are commanded to worship no other god but Him. Then in the New Testament, He stated that the greatest commandment is *Thou shalt love the Lord thy God with all thy heart, and with all thy soul, and with all thy mind* (Matthew 22:37). Our obedience should be born out of our love for God, not out of duty to a set of rules. Without love, our obedience is for naught. *If a man say, I love God, and hateth his brother, he is a liar: for he that loveth not his brother whom he hath seen, how can he love God whom he hath not seen?* (1 John 4:20). First Corinthians 13:4-7 gives us a picture of this love:

> *Charity* [love] *suffereth long, and is kind; charity envieth not; charity vaunteth* [boasts] *not itself, is not puffed up* [proud], *doth not behave itself unseemly, seeketh not her own, is not easily provoked, thinketh no evil; rejoiceth not in iniquity, but rejoiceth in the truth; beareth all things, believeth all things, hopeth all things, endureth all things.*

In addition to being a God of love, we know God is faithful. Lamentations 3:22-23 says: *It is of the LORD's mercies that we are not consumed, because his compassions fail not. They are new every morning:* **great is thy faithfulness**. God is a faithful God. Even though God may change His earthly plans for us depending on our response to Him, He will always keep His covenantal promises. He has always done what He said He will do, and He can be trusted to keep His word. Long ago, Moses told us: *Know therefore that the LORD thy God, he is God, the* ***faithful God****, which keepeth covenant and mercy with them that love him and keep his commandments to a thousand generations* (Deuteronomy 7:9). In Revelation, John says: *I saw heaven opened, and behold a white horse; and he that sat upon him was called* ***Faithful*** *and* ***True****, and in righteousness he doth judge and make war* (Revelation 19:11).

In this brief overview of God's names, we have learned that God is harsh toward sin, but incredibly loving, merciful, and gracious toward those who fear Him. The fear of God is the beginning of wisdom (Proverbs 9:10). It should make us run *to* Him, not *away* from Him. To fear God is to honor and love Him because of who He is. Our respect and love of God brings glory to His name, and He will only reveal Himself to those who love Him enough to seek Him.

I hope the names of God encourage you to study more about Him through the Scriptures. He desires to communicate with you through His written Word. Why not dedicate your life to increase your knowledge of Him? Over and over in the Bible, God says to increase your learning of Him, for only fools hate knowledge (Proverbs 1:5, 29).

Prayer

Holy Father in heaven, as You tell us in Your Word, let us not be like the wise man who glories in his wisdom. Neither let us be like the mighty man who glories in his might, nor like the rich man who glories in his riches. But if we are going to glory in anything, let us glory in the fact that we understand and know You and that You are the LORD who exercises loving kindness, judgment, and righteousness in the earth, for we were created to bring glory to Your name (Jeremiah 9:23-24).

Chapter 2

JESUS CHRIST

Christology

*But whom say ye that I [Jesus] am? And Simon
Peter answered and said, Thou art the Christ, the
Son of the living God. And Jesus answered and said
unto him, Blessed art thou, Simon Bar-jona: for
flesh and blood hath not revealed it unto thee, but
my Father which is in heaven.* (Matthew 16:15b-17)

Introduction

The study of the person and nature of Jesus Christ is called *Christology*. Christology answers the question: Who is Jesus Christ? It is not sufficient just to know *about* Jesus. The Bible tells us that *the devils also believe, and tremble* (James 2:19).

Of all the religions throughout our world, Christianity stands out as the only one whose God is a living God. All other religions worship or lift up men who have died, or they worship an idol who has never lived. Even though Jesus Christ had died, death was unable to hold Him in the grave. No other religious leader in this world possessed the power to rise from the dead or the power to forgive sin and erase guilt. Personally knowing Jesus Christ is key to your relationship with God the Father. It will also influence your understanding of the Holy Scriptures, of salvation, of the world around us, and of yourself.

What the Amish Teach

On April 21, 1632, in Dordrecht, Holland, leaders at a Dutch Mennonite conference adopted the *Dordrecht Confession of Faith*. It contains eighteen articles of faith. This document is a statement and confession of what the Anabaptists believe the Scriptures teach about major doctrines of the Bible. The views affirmed in the articles of faith are, in fact, drawn from the Holy Scriptures. Included here are a few excerpts that speak about the person of Jesus Christ.

Article 1

The belief is stated that there is "one eternal, almighty, and incomprehensible [too wonderful to understand] God, the Father, Son, and Holy Ghost, and in none more, nor in any other; before whom no God was made or existed, nor shall there be any after Him."

Later, in the second paragraph, we read, "He is the Creator of all things visible and invisible."

Article 3

The belief that with God "there was yet a means for their reconciliation [making peace], namely, the immaculate [sinless] Lamb, the Son of God, who had been foreordained [planned before] thereto before the foundation of the world . . . that He by His coming, would redeem [buy back], liberate, and raise the fallen race of man from their sin, guilt, and unrighteousness."

Article 4

On the coming of Christ into this world and His purpose we find, "the Word, Himself became flesh and man; that He was conceived in the virgin Mary, who was espoused [engaged] to a man named Joseph, of the house of David; and that she brought Him forth as her firstborn son, at Bethlehem, wrapped Him in swaddling clothes, and laid Him in a manger."

He is "God's only, first and own Son; who was before John the Baptist, before Abraham, before the world; yea, who was David's Lord, and God of the whole world, the firstborn of every creature; who was brought into the world, and to whom a body was prepared, which He yielded up as a sacrifice and offering, for a sweet savor unto God, yea, for the consolation, redemption, and salvation of all mankind. . . . He is the Son of the living God, in whom alone consist all our hope, consolation, redemption, and salvation, which we neither may nor must seek in any other. . . . [Jesus] was crucified, dead, was buried, and, on the third day, rose from the dead, and ascended to heaven; and that He sits on the right hand of God the Majesty on high, whence He will come again to judge the quick and the dead."

Martyrs Mirror, First Confession

Another Anabaptist writing held in very high regard is the *Martyrs Mirror.* This book contains many stories and incidents regarding persecution from the time of Jesus to AD 1660. Also in this book are some of the Anabaptist confessions of faith. The *Dordrecht Confession* is listed in *Martyrs Mirror* as the Third Confession. There are also two other confessions of faith listed that were prior to the one at Dordrecht. The First Confession was "drawn up at Amsterdam" on September 27, 1627, and is called "Scriptural Instruction." The Second Confession, called "Confession of Faith, and the principle articles of the Christian doctrine," is from October 7, 1630. Consider this excerpt taken from the First Confession:

> For although the blessed Lord Jesus Christ is the only meritorious [deserving] cause of the justification [made righteous] of man, their adoption by God as His children, and the foundation of their eternal salvation, God, the heavenly Father, of whom all things are, and who is the true Father of the whole family in heaven and earth, has nevertheless been pleased to impute [credit] the merits [value] of His Son Jesus Christ to man, and make him partaker of the same, through the means of faith in His beloved, only, and only-begotten Son; whereby He owns them as children, and adopts them as heirs of everlasting life, according to the testimony of John, who says: *He* (that is, Christ) *came unto his own, and his own received him not. But as many as received him, to them gave he power to become the sons of God, even to them that believe on his name: which were born, not of blood, nor of the will of the flesh, nor of the will of man, but of God* (John 1:11-13).

In both the *Dordrecht Confession of Faith* and *Martyrs Mirror*, the statements regarding the person and work of Jesus Christ are accurate. The problem arises, however, not so much in what is written, but in our understanding of what is written. It is important that our relationship with Him becomes much more than a distant association (connection) with a figure from the Bible and written about by others.

The above statements tell us that our eternal destiny, heaven

or hell, rests solely in and on the person and work of Jesus Christ.
Do we really believe what we say we believe?

Some important points to notice:

First, according to the articles of faith, Jesus Christ
is the Son of the living God, in whom alone rests
all our hope of salvation. We must know Jesus.

The second point is taken from *Martyrs Mirror*.
Jesus Christ is the only meritorious (deserving)
cause of justification (being made right). It is His
righteousness that is imputed (attributed, given) to
us, but that comes only by knowing and accepting
Him and the finished work on the cross. It is the
free gift of grace.

So often, what we say we believe is not shown in the way we
live. This is the difference between knowing *about* Jesus and
entering into a personal relationship with our living Savior.
Knowing about Jesus amounts to facts we learn about a historical figure. This type of knowledge doesn't always change our
lives. Knowing Jesus moves Him from our head to our hearts
and dramatically impacts our lives.

As we turn to the Holy Word of God for the full identity of
Jesus Christ, we find it to be very clear regarding Jesus Christ
and the importance of knowing Him. While articles of faith
and other religious documents offer much good information,
God's Word is the only truth that has not been distorted by the
corruption of the fall of man recorded in Genesis chapter 3.

What the Scriptures Teach

Jesus Christ as the Second Person of the Trinity – the Son of God

> In the beginning was the Word, and the Word was with God, and the Word was God. The same was in the beginning with God (John 1:1-2).

We discussed God the Father in the first chapter and will be discussing God the Spirit in the next chapter. God the Son, as part of the Trinity, has always existed, just as the Father and the Holy Spirit have. As part of the *Godhead* (the Trinity), Jesus is the eternal Son of God. He always was and always will be. *For in him dwelleth all the fulness of the Godhead bodily* (Colossians 2:9). He is the revelation of God. True, no man hath seen God at any time and lived (John 1:18; Exodus 33:20). God has never shown Himself without being veiled. In Christ, God was veiled in human flesh.

While on earth, Jesus spoke often about His preexistence, saying things like, *before Abraham was, I am* (John 8:58). On His last evening with His disciples, before going to the cross, He said, *And now, O Father, glorify thou me with thine own self with the glory which I had with thee before the world was* (John 17:5). Even John the Baptist bore *witness of him, and cried, saying, This was he of whom I spake, He that cometh after me is preferred before me: for he was before me* (John 1:15). The writer of the Gospel of John wrote, *And I saw, and bare record that **this is the Son of God*** (John 1:34).

Even before His human birth, Jesus enjoyed a father/son relationship with God the Father. John emphasized the importance of this relationship between God and His Son by restating that the *Word was **with** God*. God and Jesus, along with the Holy Spirit, are perfectly one in purpose, in power, and in character. *If ye had known me, ye should have known my Father also: and from henceforth ye know him, and have seen him. Philip saith unto him, Lord, shew us the Father, and it sufficeth us. Jesus saith unto him, Have I been so long time with you, and yet hast thou not known me, Philip? he that hath seen me hath seen the Father; and how sayest thou then, Shew us the Father? Believest thou not that I am in the Father, and the Father in me? the words that I speak unto you I speak not of myself: but the Father that dwelleth in me, he doeth the works* (John 14:7-10). This is similar to what a perfect marriage should look like, that while the husband and wife are separate human beings, they are so aligned and in communion that they are one unit. Take a look at chapter 17 of the Gospel of John, and you will see a beautiful, intimate prayer that the Son prayed to His Father, revealing their perfect relationship.

Jesus Christ Is Creator of the Universe

All things were made by him; and without him was not anything made that was made (John 1:3). *For by him* [Jesus] *were all things created, that are in heaven, and that are in earth, visible and invisible, whether they be thrones, or dominions, or principalities, or powers: all things were created by him, and for him* (Colossians 1:16).

The truth of God's Word leaves no question that the Father created all things through His Son. Not only was Jesus allowed to create all things, but the Father also gave Him authority over all things. Hebrews 1:1-3 says it this way: *God, who at sundry times and in divers manners spake in time past unto the fathers by the prophets, hath in these last days spoken unto us by his Son, whom he hath appointed heir of all things, by whom also he made the worlds; Who being the brightness of his glory, and the express image of his person, and* **upholding all things by the word of his power.**

The resurrected Jesus confirmed this fact before He ascended to heaven, saying, *All power is given unto me in heaven and in earth* (Matthew 28:18). He demonstrated this power over creation with His signs and miracles while on earth. He calmed a great wind storm (Mark 4:39-41), and *the men marveled, saying, What manner of man is this, that even the winds and the sea obey him!* (Matthew 8:27). Jesus even proved His authority over the spiritual world when he came into the country of the Gergesenes, where He cast demons out of a man. These demons recognized Jesus as the Son of God and that He had authority over them. The demons *cried out, saying, What have we to do with thee, Jesus, thou Son of God? Art thou come hither to torment us before the time?* (Matthew 8:29).

Jesus Was Born of God and Born of a Woman

And the Word was made flesh, and dwelt among us (John 1:14). The *incarnation* is the word we use to describe the Son of God being made flesh in the body of Jesus. He *is the* [visible] *image of the invisible God, the firstborn of every creature* (Colossians 1:15). Each born again person becomes a son or daughter of God (John 1:12), but Jesus is the *first* Son, the only begotten of God, and has privileges over us. He is higher in rank. *Wherefore God also hath highly exalted him, and given him a name which is above every name* (Philippians 2:9).

Jesus' mysterious and miraculous birth, which is humanly impossible to explain, was foretold from Genesis to the Gospels. *Behold, a virgin shall be with child, and shall bring forth a son, and they shall call his name Emmanuel, which being interpreted is, God with us* (Matthew 1:23). Every prophecy of His birth came to pass exactly as the Father said it would. The virgin birth of Jesus Christ is not to be treated lightly. It proves His deity (that He is one with God) and His humanity (that He came as a man). This is yet another mystery we do not necessarily need to fully understand to believe.

The incarnation made it possible for man to see, touch, and experience God up close – at least for those who lived during His lifetime on earth. Jesus said in John 8:18-19, *I am one that bear witness of myself, and the Father that sent me beareth witness of me . . . if ye had known me, ye should have known my Father also.* But we don't need to see and touch Him to experience and know Him. Many who saw Jesus in that day still did not believe He was the Son of God (John 6:36), but *blessed are they that have not seen, and yet have believed* (John 20:29). He is God's *Word*, and we can know Him personally by asking the Spirit to reveal Him to us as we read the Holy Scriptures.

Even though Jesus is one with God, He willingly submitted to the will and authority of His Father to function as the Son, saying, *For I came down from heaven, not to do mine own will, but the will of him that sent me* (John 6:38). His earthly parents had a hard time dealing with the fact that He was under the authority of His heavenly Father when, at a young age He said, *I must work the works of him that sent me* (John 9:4). Yet, as a child, He submitted to the fifth commandment by obeying His parents (Luke 2:51), experiencing humanity in its fullest, with all its limitations. *Who, being in the form of God, thought it not robbery to be equal with God: But made himself of no reputation and took upon him the form of a servant, and was made in the likeness of men: And being found in fashion as a man, he humbled himself, and became obedient unto death, even the death of the cross* (Philippians 2:6-8).

Can you imagine Jesus holding back His godly powers in order to identify with our humanity? Spiritually, He voluntarily became poor so that we could become rich with eternal life. *For ye know the grace of our Lord Jesus Christ, that, though he was rich, yet for your sakes he became poor, that ye through his poverty might be rich* (2 Corinthians 8:9). Jesus became a man and walked among us as a man. He experienced all the trials, temptations, and tribulations we experience in our daily lives. He overcame all of them without ever giving in to sin, and He was crucified on the cross as a sinful man. He obeyed every command laid out in the Old Testament law. He was the only perfect man to walk among us, but He died as one who had broken the law. He was a man who could *be touched with the feeling of our infirmities; but was in all points tempted like as we are, yet without sin* (Hebrews 4:15). He knows and understands our pain and helplessness. He suffered humanity in order to make us free from it.

Jesus Is Our Example

When the Bible says that Jesus is the *firstborn of every creature* (Colossians 1:15), it also means that He is the first man born who is the example of God's purpose for man. Jesus showed us what a real man is – what Adam was created to be. Jesus was the only righteous person to ever walk this earth – the only human being able to keep the whole law. He was a leader, a guide to others, and a counselor. He had more wisdom than Solomon and always told the truth, yet made himself a servant of all. He showed us what could be done by man when under the control of the Holy Spirit. It is impossible to cover all the wonderful truths of Jesus Christ in this one chapter. Yet as a man, Jesus demonstrated all the beauty and perfection of the Godhead, as listed in Galatians 5:22-23: *But the fruit of the Spirit is love, joy, peace, longsuffering, gentleness, goodness, faith, meekness, temperance: against such there is no law.* All of them can be summed up into one word – love. God's love is so powerful that it is considered the one quality Jesus said would prove to the world who His true disciples were. *By this shall all men know that ye are my disciples, if ye have love one to another* (John 13:35). His incarnation showed the image of God to mankind – what we were created to be but could not be without His Spirit within us.

Jesus Is the Redeemer of Mankind

His earthly name *Jesus* was a common name. It is the same as the Hebrew name *Joshua*, and its meaning, *God saves*, is very fitting. The word *redeem* means *to buy back*. By offering His own body on the cross, He paid the sin debt of death for all mankind. That is why we can give *thanks unto the Father . . . who hath delivered us from the power of darkness, and hath translated us into the kingdom of his dear Son: In whom we have redemption through his blood, even the forgiveness of sins* (Colossians 1:12-14).

Jesus could never have accomplished man's redemption if He had not been born into the human race. God's law demanded a blood sacrifice to atone for the sins of mankind. Only as a perfect law-keeper could He have satisfied God's demand for redemption. As God, He is eternal and could not have been killed on the cross without a body of flesh and blood.

Jesus' role as Redeemer was proved by His resurrection from the dead. The Father accepted Jesus' death in our place. To the Jewish leaders, Peter said, *The God of our fathers raised up Jesus, whom ye slew and hanged on a tree. Him hath God exalted with his right hand to be a Prince and a Saviour, for to give repentance to Israel* [and to us], *and forgiveness of sins* (Acts 5:30-31). The story of Ruth in the Bible is a beautiful picture of our redemption through Christ.

Jesus Is High Priest

Under the Old Testament law, God could only be approached by man through an animal sacrifice. The high priest's job was

to make atonement for the nation of Israel – first for themselves, then for the people. This atonement was good for only
one year at a time. It had to be repeated year after year until the
Son of God arrived. *But this man* [Jesus], *because he continueth
ever* [is eternal] *hath an unchangeable priesthood . . . seeing he
ever liveth to make intercession* [mediation] *for them. . . . Who
needeth not daily . . . to offer up sacrifice . . . for this he did once,
when he offered up himself* (Hebrews 7:24-27). Jesus did not
need to atone for His own sin, and as the perfect Lamb of God
His sacrifice endures forever, leaving no further need for the
animal atonements. Under the New Testament, we are free to
approach God without an animal sacrifice, because God the
Father was satisfied with the atoning power of Christ's sacrifice.

As High Priest, Jesus Christ is our mediator. He is a go-
between to bring peace between two parties, as stated in 1
Timothy 2:5: *For there is one God, and one mediator between
God and men, the man Christ Jesus.* As mediator, He is also our
advocate. An advocate speaks on behalf of the people he repre-
sents. So when Satan goes before God to condemn believers, as
he did with Job, Jesus reminds him that He has atoned for their
sin and has clothed them in His own righteousness, making
them acceptable before God. He freed them from Satan's power.
*And if any man sin, we have an advocate with the Father, Jesus
Christ the righteous* (1 John 2:1).

Jesus Is Head of the Church
As head of the Church, Jesus is its authority. *And hath put all
things under his feet, and gave him to be the head over all things
to the church* (Ephesians 1:22). Believers must follow His instructions for the purpose of the local church and for Christian
living, putting Jesus first in everything they do. For *he is the
head of the body, the church: who is the beginning, the firstborn
from the dead; that in all things he might have the preeminence*

[first place] (Colossians 1:18). Through Christ, God is glorified by the Church. *Unto him be glory in the church by Christ Jesus throughout all ages, world without end. Amen* (Ephesians 3:21). He is the living Savior and the object of the Church's worship. He loves the Church as a man should love his wife. He gave His eternal life to the Church. His desire is to find the Church loyal to only Him at His coming, as a chaste virgin.

Jesus Is King and Judge

The Bible talks about many kingdoms. For example: God's rule over all the earth, which Satan disrupted; His rule over the Jewish nation, which He had to set aside for the time being; His rule over the Church; and His future earthly and heavenly rule, which is foretold: *He shall be great, and shall be called the Son of the Highest: and the Lord God shall give unto him the throne of his father David; and he shall reign over the house of Jacob for ever; and of his kingdom there shall be no end* (Luke 1:32-33).

Jesus spoke of this kingship before Pilate. *Thou sayest that I am a king. To this end was I born, and for this cause came I into the world* (John 18:37). Romans 8:34 says that after Christ rose from the dead, He went to sit *at the right hand of God*, His kingly seat. That showed that Satan's reign was overthrown – another purpose of the incarnation. Even his title, Messiah or Christ, is translated as the *anointed one*, referring to His kingship.

Christ's restored kingdom over the earth will begin upon His return to earth. He will come again as a man in His glorified body. *This same Jesus, which is taken up from you into heaven, shall so come* [return] *in like manner as ye have seen him go into heaven* (Acts 1:11). It will be fulfilled as it says in Revelation: *And I saw heaven opened, and behold a white horse; and he that sat upon him was called Faithful and True, and in righteousness he doth judge and make war. . . . And he was clothed with a vesture dipped in blood: and his name is called The Word of God* (Revelation 19:11, 13).

As king, Christ will destroy His enemies and this earth with wars and judgments. And, as judge, He will judge whether the souls of men are loyal to Him by faith in the gospel, divide the tares from the wheat, and declare who spends eternity in heaven and who in hell. *Because he hath appointed a day, in the which he will judge the world in righteousness by that man [Jesus] whom he hath ordained; whereof he hath given assurance unto all men, in that he hath raised him from the dead* (Acts 17:31). The resurrection of Christ proves that the redemption of man was completed – the atonement was accepted – and *that* is what gives assurance to all believers that they will be raised to meet the Lord and received by God in the end. Hallelujah!

Conclusion

Without the virgin birth, Jesus would be just another man. Without His shed blood, we would still be separated forever from God the Father. Without the resurrection, Jesus would be dead, and His death would be useless to give us grace. Never before, nor after, in the history of our world has one man been able to cause such transformation in the lives of mankind. Of course, this is no earthly transformation. This is a supernatural change in the heart of each one who places his trust in Jesus Christ for salvation. Jesus is the only one able to give us real life, because He is the giver of life. Oh, may we have the same goal that the apostle Paul had in Philippians 3:10, *that I may know him, and the power of his resurrection.*

Prayer

Father God, we come before You with thankful hearts. Thank You for the amazing gift of eternal life through Your Son, Jesus Christ. Thank You for opening the way to come before You in prayer through the blood and body of Jesus. As we read and study Your Word, open our hearts to know Jesus in a personal way. Write Your truths and the depth of Your riches deep in our hearts. Help us in our unbelief. Father, grant us a spirit of wisdom and revelation in our knowledge of You and Your Son, Jesus Christ. Open the eyes of our hearts, so that we might know the hope of Your calling and the glorious riches of our inheritance through Your Son. Give us eyes to see the exceeding greatness of Your power toward us and the working of Your mighty power when You raised Jesus from the dead and seated Him at Your right hand forever. Amen.

Chapter 3

THE HOLY SPIRIT

Pneumatology

Howbeit when he, the Spirit of truth, is come, he will guide you into all truth: for he shall not speak of himself; but whatsoever he shall hear, that shall he speak: and he will shew you things to come. (John 16:13)

Introduction

When learning about the person of the Holy Spirit, it is important to consider what we were taught about the Father, Son, and Holy Spirit in our Amish upbringing. In some Christian circles, these three are referred to as the Holy Trinity. John wrote: *For there are three that bear record in heaven, the Father, the Word, and the Holy Ghost: and these three are one* (1 John 5:7).

What the Amish Teach

Growing up in an Old Order Amish community, our parents took us to church every other Sunday. We learned a lot about our Father in heaven, and we learned about Jesus, God's only

Son, who died on the cross, was buried, and rose from the grave three days later.

As for the Holy Spirit, He was hardly mentioned at home during prayer times or in church. Sometimes we heard about Him on the day we were baptized in the name of the Father, Son, and Holy Ghost. The Holy Spirit seemed of little to no value in our everyday lives, maybe because He is most often numbered as the third person in the Trinity.

However, Article 1 of the *Mennonite Confession of Faith* says, "We believe in the deity and personality of the Holy Spirit: that He convinces the world of sin, of righteousness, and of the judgment; that He indwells and comforts believers, guides them into all truth, empowers them and bestows certain gifts upon them for service as He wills, and enables them to live lives of righteousness."

Like most Amish families, we read our morning and evening prayers from a book, written by our forefathers. The German words, which were often difficult to understand, were spoken directly to the Father. And just like our church services, family prayer times seemed mostly boring and had little to no impact on our lives. Later in life, some of us realized the missing ingredient in our church services and family prayer times was the Holy Spirit and His power.

Until then, we didn't know that the Holy Spirit took Jesus' place at the end of His ministry. *And I will pray the Father, and he shall give you another Comforter, that he may abide with you for ever; Even the Spirit of truth; whom the world cannot receive, because it seeth him not, neither knoweth him: but ye know him; for he dwelleth with you, and shall be in you* (John 14:16-17). We didn't know that the Holy Spirit plays an active role in one's second birth.

Jesus answered and said unto him, Verily, verily, I

*say unto thee, Except a man be born again, he can-
not see the kingdom of God. Nicodemus saith unto
him, How can a man be born when he is old? can
he enter the second time into his mother's womb,
and be born? Jesus answered, Verily, verily, I say
unto thee, Except a man be born of water and of
the Spirit, he cannot enter into the kingdom of God.
That which is born of the flesh is flesh; and that
which is born of the Spirit is spirit.* (John 3:3-6)

We didn't know that the Holy Spirit dwells in the body of the
believer, empowers and equips the believer to overcome sin,
and leads him in all truth every day. *Know ye not that ye are
the temple of God, and that the Spirit of God dwelleth in you?*
(1 Corinthians 3:16).

After being born again, some see our desperate need to
understand who this Holy Spirit is and how He plays a huge
role in our daily lives as Christians. We can find our guidance
and answers when we turn to the Scriptures.

What the Scriptures Teach

Real prayer in the Spirit requires getting together with God
and speaking from your heart from the deepest parts of your
soul, not reading from a prayer book. *Praying always with all
prayer and supplication in the Spirit* (Ephesians 6:18). *But ye,
beloved, building up yourselves on your most holy faith, praying
in the Holy Ghost* (Jude 20).

Real Christians, those born of the Spirit, are given divine
and supernatural power from above. It is possible to sense the
holy presence of God. Consider the following words from Acts
4:31-33:

And when they had prayed, the place was shaken

*where they were assembled together; and they were
all filled with the Holy Ghost, and they spake the
word of God with boldness. And the multitude of
them that believed were of one heart and of one
soul. . . . And with great power gave the apostles witness of the resurrection of the Lord Jesus: and great
grace was upon them all.*

Today, many church-going people have given up the idea that
anything like this could ever happen in our generation. It is
not happening, because churchgoers do not believe. Two factors
affect churches in America, hindering our experience with the
Holy Spirit's power and continued revival:

1. We refrain from talking much about the Holy Spirit
   and His power to avoid the risk of being mistaken
   as fanatics.

2. Because God has blessed America with an abundance of financial gain, we fail to wait on the Spirit
   for our needs when we have money to get the job
   done our way.

First, let's consider the situation that took place in Acts chapter
8, where a man named Simon tried to buy Holy Spirit power:

*And when Simon saw that through laying on of the
apostles' hands the Holy Ghost was given, he offered
them money, saying, Give me also this power, that
on whomsoever I lay hands, he may receive the Holy
Ghost.*

*But Peter said unto him, Thy money perish with
thee, because thou hast thought that the gift of God
may be purchased with money. Thou hast neither
part nor lot in this matter: for thy heart is not right
in the sight of God. (Acts 8:18-21)*

Obviously, Simon had witnessed the working of the Holy Spirit, but when the apostle Paul met with some church members in Ephesus and the conversation turned to the Holy Spirit, they replied, *We have not so much as heard whether there be any Holy Ghost* (Acts 19:2). This statement from the Ephesian disciples concerning the Holy Spirit illustrates the sad and shameful treatment often given Him, even in our day. Far too often, the Holy Spirit's existence has been ignored and His ministry misunderstood. Therefore, we need to shed light on the Holy Spirit – who He is, what He does in our world, and how He fits into our everyday Christian lives.

We must remember that when the Holy Spirit does something, God is at work – creating, speaking, transforming us, living within us, and working in and through us. Although the Holy Spirit can do this work without us knowing, it is helpful for us to know more; otherwise, we end up in the same place Israel did. *My people are destroyed for lack of knowledge* (Hosea 4:6).

Whenever the Holy Spirit is involved in our lives, God is working. For example, when Ananias lied in Acts 5, we are told that he lied to the Holy Spirit, and then it says, *Thou hast not lied unto men, but unto God* (Acts 5:4). Ananias wasn't lying to a representative of God. He was lying to God.

When a lost, hell-bound sinner believes upon the name of the Lord to be saved, many wonderful things take place. That individual is instantly forgiven of all his sins, translated from death to life, removed from the kingdom of Satan, and placed into God's kingdom. But here is the most amazing part – the Father and Son, in the person of the Holy Spirit, move in to dwell inside every believer. *As God hath said, I will dwell in them, and walk in them; and I will be their God, and they shall be my people* (2 Corinthians 6:16). The moment we believe, Jesus comes into our lives. We become a living, walking, breathing temple, and the Spirit of God dwells inside us. Jesus said, *Even the Spirit of truth; whom the world cannot receive, because it seeth him not, neither knoweth him: but ye know him; for he dwelleth with you, and shall be in you* (John 14:17). Later, the apostle Paul wrote: *Know ye not that ye are the temple of God, and that the Spirit of God dwelleth in you?* (1 Corinthians 3:16).

In the Old Testament, the Spirit of God came upon people and anointed them for service. This is how He inspired the Old Testament prophets to write the Scriptures, but this anointing was temporary. In the New Testament, the Lord indwells people through the new birth, and they become His permanent abode.

Appearance of the Holy Spirit

Most people think of the Holy Spirit as being an invisible force. They think of Him as being untouchable and as some type of powerful energy that rules the universe. However, in Scripture the Holy Spirit is referred to as a dove (John 1:32), fire (Acts 2:3), oil (Luke 4:18), cloud (Exodus 33:9), voice (Psalm 95:7; Matthew 10:20), water (John 7:37-39), wind (John 3:8), and breath (John 20:21-23).

Deity of the Holy Spirit

While the Holy Spirit is overlooked in many Christian gatherings, it is important for true believers to recognize that when the Holy Spirit dwells in us, God dwells in us. Consider the fact that when we are born again, the Holy Spirit abides in us, as we saw in John 14:17. And, Christ is in us. *To whom God would make known what is the riches of the glory of this mystery among the Gentiles; which is Christ in you, the hope of glory* (Colossians 1:27). First John 4:12 also tells us that God is in us: *No man hath seen God at any time. If we love one another, God dwelleth in us, and his love is perfected in us.* That abiding presence is God Himself, the Three in One, and the source of eternal life.

God the Spirit is equal to the Father and the Son and possesses the same characteristics:

He is everywhere at all times. David wrote: *Whither shall I go from thy spirit? or whither shall I flee from thy presence?* (Psalm 139:7).

He is all-seeing and all-knowing. *But God hath revealed them unto us by his Spirit: for the Spirit searcheth all things, yea, the deep things of God. For what man knoweth the things of a man, save the spirit of man which is in him? even so the things of God knoweth no man, but the Spirit of God* (1 Corinthians 2:10-11).

He is all-powerful and unstoppable. *And the earth was without form, and void; and darkness was upon the face of the deep. And the Spirit of God moved upon the face of the waters* (Genesis 1:2).

He has no beginning and no end. *How much more shall the blood of Christ, who through the eternal Spirit offered himself without spot to God, purge your conscience from dead works to serve the living God?* (Hebrews 9:14).

The Person of the Holy Spirit

It is easy to think of the Holy Spirit as a vague presence if you do not understand that He is a Person in the sense that the Father is a Person and the Son is a Person. Scripture shows us He has feelings. We know the Holy Spirit can be grieved (sorely disappointed), because Paul says, *Grieve not the holy Spirit of God, whereby ye are sealed unto the day of redemption* (Ephesians 4:30); we have already seen with Ananias that He can be lied to (Acts 5:3). Paul also tells us to *quench* [smother] *not the Spirit* (1 Thessalonians 5:19), and Stephen accused the Jews when he said, *Ye do always resist the Holy Ghost* (Acts 7:51). Jesus told the people that *the blasphemy* [denying, cursing] *against the Holy Ghost shall not be forgiven unto men* (Matthew 12:31). In Hebrews, we read of the insults flung at the Son of God: *Of how much sorer punishment, suppose ye, shall he be thought worthy, who hath trodden under foot the Son of God, and hath counted the blood of the covenant, wherewith he was sanctified, an unholy thing, and hath done despite unto the Spirit of grace?* (Hebrews 10:29). So we see that the Spirit can be grieved, lied to, quenched, resisted, blasphemed, and insulted.

Author of the Old and New Testaments

In Old Testament times, the Holy Spirit came upon certain people for a specific reason. When that reason was fulfilled, the Holy Spirit departed. *Then Samuel took the horn of oil, and anointed him in the midst of his brethren: and the Spirit of the LORD came upon David from that day forward. So Samuel rose up, and went to Ramah. But the Spirit of the LORD departed from Saul* (1 Samuel 16:13-14). King David recognized this aspect of the Holy Spirit's ministry in the Old Testament and prayed: *Cast me not away from thy presence; and take not thy holy spirit from me* (Psalm 51:11).

Peter explains that the Old Testament was written by men moved by the Holy Spirit. *For the prophecy came not in old time by the will of man: but holy men of God spake as they were moved by the Holy Ghost* (2 Peter 1:21). David agreed, saying, *The Spirit of the LORD spake by me, and his word was in my tongue* (2 Samuel 23:2). Jeremiah also wrote: *Then the LORD put forth his hand, and touched my mouth. And the LORD said unto me, Behold, I have put my words in thy mouth* (Jeremiah 1:9).

This same mystery also brought us the New Testament. John wrote: *He that hath an ear, let him hear what the Spirit saith unto the churches: To him that overcometh will I give to eat of the tree of life, which is in the midst of the paradise of*

God (Revelation 2:7). Paul wrote: *Which things also we speak, not in the words which man's wisdom teacheth, but which the Holy Ghost teacheth; comparing spiritual things with spiritual* (1 Corinthians 2:13).

The Holy Spirit's Ministry

The Person of the Holy Spirit was already present and active in the work of creation, as seen in the second verse of Genesis. *And the earth was without form, and void; and darkness was upon the face of the deep. And the Spirit of God moved upon the face of the waters* (Genesis 1:2).

In Numbers 11, the people of Israel were complaining. When Moses turned to God with his problem, God told him to choose seventy men from the elders of Israel and bring them to Him. *And I will come down and talk with thee there: and I will take of the spirit which is upon thee, and will put it upon them; and they shall bear the burden of the people with thee, that thou bear it not thyself alone* (Numbers 11:17). In verse 25, this was accomplished: *And the LORD came down in a cloud, and spake unto him, and took of the spirit that was upon him, and gave it unto the seventy elders: and it came to pass, that, when the spirit rested upon them, they prophesied, and did not cease.*

In 1 Samuel 11:6, *the Spirit of God came upon Saul* in power, and in 1 Samuel 16:14, *the Spirit of the LORD departed from Saul, and an evil spirit from the LORD troubled him.*

In the New Testament, the Holy Spirit was involved throughout Jesus' life on earth. The Spirit placed Jesus in Mary's womb and *the angel of the LORD appeared unto him* [Joseph] *in a dream, saying, Joseph, thou son of David, fear not to take unto thee Mary thy wife: for that which is conceived in her is of the Holy Ghost* (Matthew 1:20). He descended on Jesus at baptism: *and lo, the heavens were opened unto him, and he saw the Spirit of God descending like a dove, and lighting upon him* (Matthew

3:16). *And Jesus being full of the Holy Ghost returned from Jordan, and was led by the Spirit into the wilderness* (Luke 4:1). And then, a most amazing thing happened when Jesus was in the synagogue. He opened the book of Isaiah and said, *The Spirit of the Lord is upon me, because he hath anointed me to preach the gospel* (Luke 4:18).

It was through the Spirit of God that Jesus drove out demons. *But if I cast out devils by the Spirit of God, then the kingdom of God is come unto you* (Matthew 12:28). By that same Spirit, Jesus was raised from the dead. *But if the Spirit of him that raised up Jesus from the dead dwell in you, he that raised up Christ from the dead shall also quicken your mortal bodies by his Spirit that dwelleth in you* (Romans 8:11).

The night Jesus met with Nicodemus, He taught Nicodemus that no man can enter the kingdom of God unless he is *born of water and of the Spirit* (John 3:5). Jesus also taught: *If any man thirst, let him come unto me, and drink. He that believeth on me, as the scripture hath said, out of his belly shall flow rivers of living water* (John 7:37-38). John adds an explanation concerning the rivers of living water: *But this spake he of the Spirit, which they that believe on Him should receive* (John 7:39).

At age thirty, Jesus went into full-time ministry. People followed Him and listened to His teachings. Many of His followers thought He was the one who would deliver them from the Roman government and be their next king. What a surprise when Jesus said, *Ye have heard how I said unto you, I go away . . . because I said, I go unto the Father* (John 14:28). Jesus' disciples were dumbfounded. In one short moment, their whole world turned upside down.

- They had given up everything and followed Jesus.

- He had taught them for three years.

- They knew no other master.

- Peter said he would give his own life for Him.

- Thomas asked Jesus to let them go with Him.

In Jesus' final discourse to His disciples, we see numerous promises He would fulfill on their behalf. In John 14:15-26, we find the core of His message. He told them that after His departure, the Holy Spirit would come in His place:

> *If ye love me, keep my commandments. And I will pray the Father, and he shall give you another Comforter, that he may abide with you for ever; Even the Spirit of truth; whom the world cannot receive, because it seeth him not, neither knoweth him: but ye know him; for he dwelleth with you, and shall be in you. I will not leave you comfortless: I will come to you.*

> *Yet a little while, and the world seeth me no more; but ye see me: because I live, ye shall live also. At that day ye shall know that I am in my Father, and ye in me, and I in you.*

> *He that hath my commandments, and keepeth them, he it is that loveth me: and he that loveth me shall be loved of my Father, and I will love him, and will manifest myself to him.*

> *Judas saith unto him, not Iscariot, Lord, how is it that thou wilt manifest thyself unto us, and not unto the world?*

> *Jesus answered and said unto him, If a man love me, he will keep my words: and my Father will love him, and we will come unto him, and make our abode with him. He that loveth me not keepeth not my sayings: and the word which ye hear is not mine,*

but the Father's which sent me. These things have I spoken unto you, being yet present with you.

But the Comforter, which is the Holy Ghost, whom the Father will send in my name, he shall teach you all things, and bring all things to your remembrance, whatsoever I have said unto you.

This brings us to John 16:7, where Jesus makes a powerful statement about the coming Holy Spirit: *It is expedient for you* [to your advantage or for your own good] *that I go away: for if I go not away, the Comforter* [Holy Spirit] *will not come unto you; but if I depart, I will send him unto you.* These were meant to be words of encouragement to His disciples: "Look, it is for your advantage that I leave, because as soon as I leave, I'll send the Holy Spirit in my place." Why was it to our advantage that Jesus left and sent the Holy Spirit?

Jesus was on earth as a man and could only be at one place at a time. However, the Spirit could be everywhere at the same time.

Jesus ministered to people from the outside in, whereas the Holy Spirit ministers to people from the inside out.

When the Spirit showed up in Acts chapter 2, more happened in a few hours than happened in Jesus' three years of ministry. Since that time, tens of thousands of Holy Spirit empowered missionaries have been sent throughout the world. As a result, millions of lost souls have been brought into the kingdom of God.

Holy Spirit's Role in the New Birth

We are *by nature the children of wrath* (Ephesians 2:3). In Psalm 51:5, David says, *Behold, I was shapen in iniquity; and in sin did my mother conceive me.* We come into the world and from the beginning are bent on being independent from God and running after the things of the world. Something has to happen to us if we are to be saved from the wrath of God (1 Thessalonians 1:10). We must be changed. Therefore, the Holy Spirit *will reprove* [convict] *the world of sin, and of righteousness, and of judgment* (John 16:8).

The new birth is the result of the work of the Holy Spirit enabling us to see our sin as God sees it and to see our desperate need for a Savior. The Holy Spirit quickens (makes alive) a spiritually dead person. *It is the spirit that quickeneth; the flesh profiteth nothing* (John 6:63). Paul wrote: *The letter killeth, but the spirit giveth life* (2 Corinthians 3:6). When a spiritually dead person is made alive (born again), the Holy Spirit:

Seals the believer

In whom also after that ye believed, ye were sealed with that holy Spirit of promise. (Ephesians 1:13)

And grieve not the holy Spirit of God, whereby ye are sealed unto the day of redemption. (Ephesians 4:30)

Nevertheless the foundation of God standeth sure, having this seal, The Lord knoweth them that are his. (2 Timothy 2:19)

Empowers the believer

But ye shall receive power, after that the Holy Ghost is come upon you. (Acts 1:8)

For the law of the Spirit of life in Christ Jesus hath made me free from the law of sin and death. (Romans 8:2)

Is the earnest (guarantee) of the believer

In whom ye also trusted, after that ye heard the word of truth, the gospel of your salvation: in whom also after that ye believed, ye were sealed with that holy Spirit of promise, which is the earnest of our inheritance until the redemption of the purchased possession, unto the praise of his glory. (Ephesians 1:13-14)

Is promised to reside in us

Even the Spirit of truth; whom the world cannot receive, because it seeth him not, neither knoweth him: but ye know him; for he dwelleth with you and shall be in you. (John 14:17)

To whom God would make known what is the riches of the glory of this mystery among the Gentiles; which is Christ in you, the hope of glory. (Colossians 1:27)

Becomes the believer's partner in prayer

Likewise the Spirit also helpeth our infirmities: for we know not what we should pray for as we ought: but the Spirit itself maketh intercession for us with groanings which cannot be uttered. And he that searcheth the hearts knoweth what is the mind of the Spirit, because he maketh intercession for the saints according to the will of God. (Romans 8:26-27)

The Holy Spirit as Gift-Giver

Gifts of the Spirit are special abilities given by the Holy Spirit to believers for the purpose of building up the body of Christ. The list of spiritual gifts in 1 Corinthians 12:8-10 includes wisdom, knowledge, faith, healing, miracles, prophecy, discerning of spirits, speaking in tongues, and interpretation of tongues. Similar lists appear in Ephesians 4:7-13 and Romans 12:3-8 and include apostles, prophets, evangelists, pastors, and teachers.

The gifts of the Spirit are simply God enabling believers

to do what He has called us to do. Ephesians 4:12-14 says He gave those gifts *for the perfecting of the saints, for the work of the ministry, for the edifying of the body of Christ: Till we all come in the unity of the faith, and of the knowledge of the Son of God, unto a perfect man, unto the measure of the stature of the fulness of Christ: That we henceforth be no more children, tossed to and fro, and carried about with every wind of doctrine, by the sleight of men, and cunning craftiness, whereby they lie in wait to deceive.*

Regarding the supernatural gifts of the Spirit, we must be aware of two things. First, the supernatural gifts have long been the subject of controversy in Christian circles. They have caused family members to turn against each other and churches to divide. Some Christians believe and teach that certain gifts (speaking in tongues, interpretation of tongues, prophecy, healings, and miracles) ceased after we received the New Testament in written form (1 Corinthians 13:10). Others believe and teach that all the gifts are in operation, just like they were in the early church.

Secondly, some believers have become so caught up in the supernatural gifts that they have thrown out the foundational doctrines of the Bible. Additionally, they have made a religion out of the God-given gifts and have become worshippers of the gifts rather than worshipping the Giver of the gifts. For these sad reasons, other believers have chosen to walk in the opposite direction and have quenched and suffocated the power and the supernatural gifts of the Holy Spirit.

Both approaches are off balance. Our focus ought to be to desire the best gifts, but in love. For that reason, consider the following portion of Scripture:

> *But covet earnestly the best gifts: and yet shew I unto you a more excellent way.*

Though I speak with the tongues of men and of
angels, and have not charity (love), *I am become as*
sounding brass, or a tinkling cymbal.

And though I have the gift of prophecy, and under-
stand all mysteries, and all knowledge; and though
I have all faith, so that I could remove mountains,
and have not charity, I am nothing.

And though I bestow all my goods to feed the
poor, and though I give my body to be burned,
and have not charity, it profiteth me nothing
(1 Corinthians 12:31-13:3).

How the Holy Spirit Speaks

It is quite clear from reading the Scriptures that the Holy Spirit
is able to speak like a human being, as well as speak in a still,
small voice, to our spirit. When He speaks, the Bible commands
us to listen to His voice. Consider the following instances when
the Holy Spirit showed up and spoke to mankind in the flesh:

Then the Spirit said unto Philip, Go near, and join
thyself to this chariot. (Acts 8:29)

As they [the church] *ministered to the Lord, and*
fasted, the Holy Ghost said, Separate me Barnabas
and Saul for the work whereunto I have called
them. And when they had fasted and prayed, and
laid their hands on them, they sent them away. So
they, being sent forth by the Holy Ghost, departed.
(Acts 13:2-4)

Take no thought beforehand what ye shall speak,
neither do ye premeditate [think about ahead of
time]: *but whatsoever shall be given you in that*

hour, that speak ye: for it is not ye that speak, but
the Holy Ghost. (Mark 13:11)

Walking in the Spirit

Before we were born again, we had only one nature – the fleshly
nature. Our decisions and choices were based on our own flesh
and desires. After the new birth, we should have a new nature
– being regenerated by the Holy Spirit. This simply means that
as born-again believers, we wake up in the morning and have
to choose which master we want to obey. If we choose to obey
our old fleshly self, we will often appear to others as one who
has never been born again. If we choose to obey the Spirit, we
will appear as one who has experienced the new birth. *This I
say then, Walk in the Spirit, and ye shall not fulfil the lust of
the flesh. For the flesh lusteth against the Spirit, and the Spirit
against the flesh: and these are contrary the one to the other: so
that ye cannot do the things that ye would* (Galatians 5:16-17).

Walking in the Spirit means walking in harmony with God
and others. We must guard our hearts and tongues from con-
tinuing in our old ways of bickering, bitterness, and conflict.
We must learn to rest in Him and let Him fight our battles.
Resting in God's power is a sign of true faith. If we truly walk
in the Spirit, we will find the following list of "fruit" appearing
in our everyday life: *But the fruit of the Spirit is love, joy, peace,
longsuffering, gentleness, goodness, faith, meekness, temperance: against such there is no law* (Galatians 5:22-23). The fruit
spoken of in these verses cannot be faked or manufactured
by the believer. Our part is to yield and trust. God's part is to
produce the fruit: *Abide in me, and I in you. As the branch cannot bear fruit of itself, except it abide in the vine; no more can
ye, except ye abide in me. I am the vine, ye are the branches: He*

that abideth in me, and I in him, the same bringeth forth much fruit: for without me ye can do nothing (John 15:4-5).

Prayer

Dear Lord, Thank You for sending the Holy Spirit to dwell in our bodies. Thank You for the many times He has comforted our hearts, led us in all truth, protected us from evil, and empowered us to do the work of the ministry. We stand in awe! My utmost and passionate prayer is that You, O God, would use this study to start a fire in the reader's soul. Awake us from our heavy slumber and dead religion and send a Holy Spirit revival. In Jesus' name, Amen.

Chapter 4

THE BIBLE

Bibliology

All scripture is given by inspiration of God, and is profitable for doctrine, for reproof, for correction, for instruction in righteousness: That the man of God may be perfect, throughly furnished unto all good works. (2 Timothy 3:16-17)

Introduction

Bibliology tells us what the Bible is. It is the study of how we can know that the Bible is true, that it is *all* true, and that it is inspired by God. Bibliology includes learning how we got the Bible, how we know the books included in the Bible belong in it, and why other books should not be included. The following list of terms related to Bibliology will help us better understand the rest of the chapter:

Revelation: God revealed Himself and made His Word known to us by giving us the Scriptures. He let us know what He wanted us to know.

Inspiration: The Scriptures are *God-breathed*, meaning that the Scriptures were given to us by God. What was written was intended by God to be written. None of the Bible was merely made up by man. *All scripture is given by inspiration of God* (2 Timothy 3:16).

Plenary: Entire or complete inspiration. Every part of the Bible is from God. We do not decide which parts to follow and which to ignore. All sixty-six books were given to us by the inspiration (breath) and will of God. Every original word in the Bible is inspired by God (this is also known as verbal inspiration – every word) and was written as intended and directed by God.

Inerrant and Infallible: The Scriptures as given to us by God are free from error. God made no mistakes with any of the words given to us in the Bible. We can trust the entire Bible, as it comes from God, who is Truth.

Sufficiency: What God has given to us in the Bible is sufficient, or all that we need, in order to know the way of salvation and to follow Jesus in living a holy life. One day we will see the things of God more clearly, but in this life, what God has decided in His wisdom to reveal to us in His Word is all that we need in order to learn of Him, to live for Him, and to love Him.

Authority: The Scriptures are from God Himself and are to be taken as they are – the actual Word of God – as if God were speaking directly and individually to each of us, with the full weight and power of God Himself.

Preservation: God is able to preserve His Word for us down through the ages, and He has done so. Despite many attempts to destroy the Word of God, it lives and abides forever. God has protected and maintained His Word for us. It has not changed.

What God told Moses thousands of years ago is preserved for us in the Scriptures. Thousands of ancient biblical manuscripts have been found and confirm that what was recorded in the ancient biblical writings remains the same as what we have in the Bible today.

Canon: This means *measure* or *rule*, and refers to the specific books which make up our Bible. The sixty-six books in the Bible make up the *canon* of Holy Scripture. Books are not to be added to or subtracted from the canon.

What Many Amish Believe

While the *Dordrecht Confession of Faith* does not contain a specific section explaining the importance of the Scriptures, phrases can be found throughout the Confession alluding to the reliance upon the Scriptures as the basis of belief. Phrases such as "according to the holy Scriptures," "We furthermore believe and confess with the Scriptures," "as the Scripture says," and "according to Scripture" are common in the Confession.

Martyrs Mirror is another important Anabaptist writing, providing much Anabaptist history, especially in regard to the many who suffered for their faith. The book contains many different Anabaptist confessions of faith detailing Anabaptist beliefs. One such confession can be found a few hundred pages into *Martyrs Mirror,* and is simply titled *Confession of Faith according to the Holy Word of God.* This confession is described as "a certain *Confession of Faith,* which very probably, was once contained in the *History of the pious Anabaptist Martyrs* and is declared to have been the summary of their faith," and is thought to have originated around the year 1600. Article XI of this Confession contains the following points:

The Bible Is the Written Word of God

The Bible is the "written Word of God."

The Old Testament includes the five books of Moses and "also all kings, priests, and prophets, who prophesied and spoke, through the Spirit of God, among this people, Israel."

The Old Testament is historical and also spiritual and brings us to a better hope – to Christ.

"The Levitical priesthood, ceremonies, and sacrifices, the land of Canaan, kings, the city of Jerusalem, and the Temple . . . pointed and led to Christ Jesus."

"The old law was an intolerable yoke of bondage, which brought condemnation upon all who did not continue in, and perform all that is written in the book of the law."

The Bible Is the Word of Reconciliation and Grace

The Bible can lead us to a loving relationship with God through His grace:

"Christ Jesus came, who is the end and the fulfilling of the old law."

Jesus is the "author of the new law, of perfect liberty, and the real, true light, to which all the dark shadows pointed."

Christ Jesus was "sent from God, with full power in heaven and on earth and is the one who has abolished death, and brought life and immortality to light through the Gospel."

Jesus "made a new covenant with the house of Israel . . . and has invited thereto all the Gentiles and nations of the earth" so that "by obedience through grace, they may now become fellow citizens with the saints, and of the household of God."

This is the "word of reconciliation, by which Almighty God, through His Spirit, works faith, regeneration, and all the good fruits . . . in men; in which word of the New Testament are proclaimed to us full grace and peace, forgiveness of sins, and eternal life, together with all things, that pertain unto life and godliness, yea, all the counsel of God."

Holy Scriptures Regulate and Measure Faith

All believing children of the New Testament must "regulate and conduct themselves in all matters relating to the faith; in accordance with which, finally, an eternal judgment will be held."

"This New and everlasting Covenant, which is confirmed with the precious death and blood of our Lord Jesus Christ," may "not be changed, or anything taken from or added to it . . . according to one's own individual opinions."

"All Christians are in duty bound to bow their whole heart, mind, and soul under the obedience of Christ and the mind of the Holy Spirit expressed in the holy Scriptures, and to regulate and measure their whole faith and conversation according to [its precepts]."

Man Lives by Every Word Proceeding from the Mouth of the Lord

The Old Testament is to be explained by and shown to agree with the New Testament and must be taught among the people of God, including "Moses with his stern, threatening, punishing law over all impenitent sinners as still under the law; but Christ with His new, glad tidings of the holy Gospel over all believing, penitent sinners as not under the law, but under grace."

"To this new law of Jesus Christ all decrees, councils, and ordinances made contrary to it by men in the world, must give place; but all Christians must . . . regulate and conduct themselves only in accordance with this blessed Gospel of Christ."

"As the outward man lives outwardly by the nourishment of bread; so the inward man of the soul lives by every word proceeding from the mouth of the Lord."

"Therefore, the Word of God must be purely and sincerely preached, heard, received, and kept, by all believers."

One can see that the Amish rightly place great importance on the Holy Scriptures as the Word of God, to be taught, read, believed, and lived by all who profess to follow Jesus.

What the Scriptures Teach

Moses wrote the first five books of the Bible about 3,500 years ago. John wrote the book of Revelation around AD 90-98. All thirty-nine books of the Old Testament and all twenty-seven books of the New Testament, though written over a period of more than one thousand years by about forty different people, are inspired by God and remain God's Word for us today.

The Jews had the Scriptures in their common Hebrew language with some portions in Daniel and Ezra written in Aramaic (an ancient Middle Eastern language). The first translation of the Old Testament was into Greek (called the Septuagint) around 300 BC, because many of the Jewish people could no longer read Hebrew. The New Testament was originally written in common, everyday Greek, and then in AD 382, Jerome (born Eusebius Hieronymus Sophronius) began translating the entire Bible into Latin, which was the language of ordinary Christians of the Roman Empire, giving the early church the Scriptures in their common languages of Greek or Latin.

God intended for us to have the Bible in our own common language. If our common language is German, then we would read the Bible in German. If the language we read best is English, then we should read the Bible in English. Why would God want us to read the Bible in a language we don't understand well?

People who were used by God in the Bible believed the Word of God to be true. From Moses to David to Isaiah to Jesus to the apostles, they believed Scripture to be from God – the source of truth and final authority on matters of faith and doctrine:

Moses said, *Behold, I have taught you statutes and judgments, even as the LORD my God commanded me, that ye should do so in the land whither ye go to possess it* (Deuteronomy 4:5).

In Psalm 119, the longest chapter in the entire Bible, David repeatedly wrote of his love for the Word of God and how it applied to his life. In Psalm 19:7-10, we see another example, where David wrote:

The law of the LORD is perfect, converting the soul: the testimony of the LORD is sure, making wise the simple. The statutes of the LORD are right, rejoicing the heart: the commandment of the LORD is pure, enlightening the eyes. The fear of the LORD is clean, enduring for ever: the judgments of the LORD are true and righteous altogether. More to be desired are they than gold, yea, than much fine gold: sweeter also than honey and the honeycomb.

Isaiah wrote, *Seek ye out of the book of the LORD, and read* (Isaiah 34:16). Later he said, *The grass withereth, the flower fadeth: but the word of our God shall stand for ever* (Isaiah 40:8).

The prophet Jeremiah recorded: *Is not my word like as a fire? saith the LORD; and like a hammer that breaketh the rock in pieces?* (Jeremiah 23:29).

Jesus Himself told religious leaders, *Ye do err, not knowing the scriptures, nor the power of God* (Matthew 22:29). He told His own disciples, *These are the words which I spake unto you, while I was yet with you, that all things must be fulfilled, which were written in the law of Moses, and in the prophets, and in the psalms, concerning me* (Luke 24:44).

Another side to this is that while the Bible is the holy Word of God, it itself is not God. *Search the scriptures,* Jesus said, *for in them ye think ye have eternal life: and they are they which testify* [give evidence] *of me* (John 5:39).

The Jews in Berea would not even believe the apostle Paul unless they were convinced he taught the Scriptures correctly. *These were more noble than those in Thessalonica, in that they received the word with all readiness of mind, and searched the scriptures daily, whether those things were so* (Acts 17:11).

The apostle Paul wrote much about the importance and necessity of the Word of God, including: *So then faith cometh by hearing, and hearing by the word of God* (Romans 10:17).

Paul knew the Bible was not a mere human book but was the Word of God. *For this cause also thank we God without ceasing, because, when ye received the word of God which ye heard of us, ye received it not as*

the word of men, but as it is in truth, the word of God
(1 Thessalonians 2:13).

Paul also told us that studying the Bible is part of being a good follower of Jesus. *Study to shew thyself approved unto God, a workman that needeth not to be ashamed, rightly dividing the word of truth* (2 Timothy 2:15).

Paul reminded Timothy that the Scriptures are able to teach us about salvation. *From a child thou hast known the holy scriptures, which are able to make thee wise unto salvation through faith which is in Christ Jesus* (2 Timothy 3:15).

The writer to the Hebrews tells us: *For the word of God is quick, and powerful, and sharper than any two-edged sword, piercing even to the dividing asunder of soul and spirit, and of the joints and marrow, and is a discerner of the thoughts and intents of the heart* (Hebrews 4:12).

Peter wrote that we should long for the Word so we can grow as believers. *As newborn babes, desire the sincere milk of the word, that ye may grow thereby* (1 Peter 2:2).

Peter also wrote about the role of the Word in the new birth. *Being born again, not of corruptible* [decaying] *seed, but of incorruptible* [not able to decay], *by the word of God, which liveth and abideth for ever. For all flesh is as grass, and all the glory of man as the flower of grass. The grass withereth, and the flower thereof falleth away: but the word of the Lord endureth for ever* (1 Peter 1:23-25).

This famous summary of what the Bible ought to mean to each of us was written by Paul: *All scripture is given by inspiration of God, and is profitable for doctrine, for reproof, for correction, for instruction in righteousness: That the man of God may be perfect, throughly furnished unto all good works* (2 Timothy 3:16-17).

Many more examples could also have been given from both the Old and New Testaments that not only show the importance of the Word of God in the lives of the biblical authors, but also show the significance that God's Word ought to have in our own lives. While Christians ought to meet with other believers, and church leaders should be good and godly men, notice that these verses do not tell us to rely upon religion, church, or even church leaders. Rather, we are to go to the Scriptures, study God's Word, and the Bible is to be the final authority in our lives.

God's ways are best and right. Either we accept His Word or we reject it. There can be no middle ground. Either the Bible is from God or it is not. Either it is all true or we cannot rely on any of it. As believers, we know God's Word is true – all true. It is His Word revealed to us (revelation). All Scripture is given by inspiration of God (plenary, verbal inspiration). The Scriptures, as given by God, are without error (infallible and inerrant). The Word of God is what it claims to be – the Word of God – and as such, comes with the authority of God Himself. No mere man can rightly declare God or His Word to be wrong. The sixty-six books of the Bible contain all we need to know in order to live this life and prepare for the next (sufficiency). God has preserved His Word for us, and we can know with certainty that what was written thousands of years ago is the same as what we have in the Bible today (preservation).

Historical Accuracy

It is amazing how often people doubt the truth of the Bible or deny its historical accuracy, only to see the Bible proven right again and again through archaeological, historical, or scientific evidence. For instance, prior to the late nineteenth century, nothing was known about the Hittites except for what was in the Bible. This led many Bible critics to claim that the biblical authors invented the Hittites. Based on this mistaken belief, they suggested it was proof that the Bible was not true.

Then in 1876, a British scholar named A. H. Sayce found inscriptions (writings) carved on rocks in Turkey, which he suspected might be evidence of the Hittite nation. Ten years later, more clay tablets were discovered in Turkey. German cuneiform (writing) expert Hugo Winckler investigated the tablets and began his own excavation at the site in 1906. He found five temples, a citadel (fortified center of a city), a record of a treaty between Ramesses II and the Hittite king, and more. The discovery also confirmed other biblical facts. Such evidence as this should not surprise Christians, because we who accept the Bible by faith know that it is true and that it can never be proven to be wrong, for it is from God.

Anabaptists, along with most Protestants, believe the Bible is the inspired Word of God. They respect the Bible as a special book from God. Sadly, though, many don't read it in their common language. Even though Jesus says to search the Scriptures, even though He said the religious leaders were wrong because they did not know the Scriptures or the power of God, and even though the Bible tells of the wisdom of the Berean Jews for making sure that what they were being taught was actually from the Bible, many today still rely mainly upon church teachings without studying the Scriptures on their own. They know what they believe, but they don't verify (prove) it. They can repeat what they were taught, but they can't show others what the Bible actually says about those beliefs. They rely more upon men for their beliefs than on the pure Word of God.

Examples and Illustrations

When Dr. Pollich of Mellerstadt heard Martin Luther lecture at the University of Wittenberg, he said, "That monk will confound all the learned doctors, propound a new doctrine, and reform the whole Roman church, for he studies the writings of the prophets and evangelists." He said, "He relies on the Word of Jesus Christ, and no one can subvert [overthrow] that, either with philosophy [other beliefs] or with sophistry [false or deceptive reasoning]." [1] May we, also, rely upon the Word of God.

Martin Luther said, "For some years now, I have read through the Bible twice every year. If you picture the Bible to be a mighty tree and every word a little branch, I have shaken every one of these branches because I wanted to know what it was and what it meant." Luther believed in living according to the Bible, saying, "You may as well quit reading and hearing the Word of God, and give it to the devil, if you do not desire to live according to it." May we, also, read the Bible daily and search the Scriptures for wisdom and truth.

Famous British preacher Charles Spurgeon said, "I have heard of two Romanists, a man and his wife, who became possessed of a copy of the Scriptures, of which they had never seen one before. The man began to read it, and one night, as he sat beside the fire with the open book, he said, 'Wife, if this book is right, we are wrong.' He continued reading, and a few days after this, he said, 'Wife, if this book is right, we are lost.' More eager now than ever, to see what the Word of the Lord was, he studied the book, until one night he joyfully exclaimed, "Wife, if this book is true, we are saved.'

> "The same Word that showed them they were undone [lost], revealed also the gospel of salvation. This is the glory of the Word of God; it is against us until we are led out of our sins, and then we find that death becomes the gate of life to our souls, and the Word of God is on our side. The same Word that reveals the terrors of the Lord, also says, 'He that believeth on the Son hath everlasting life.'"[2]

---

1   Gustave Ferdinand Leopold König and Heinrich Gelzer, *The Life of Luther,* 1858.
2   Charles Spurgeon, *The Complete Works of C. H. Spurgeon,* Volume 37.

How much time does it take to read from Genesis to Revelation? If you read the Bible at standard pulpit speed (slow enough to be heard and understood), the reading time would be seventy-one hours. If you break that down into minutes and divide it into 365 days, you could read the entire Bible, cover to cover, in only twelve minutes a day. Is this really too much time to spend reading about God?[3]

Catherine Booth, wife of the founder of the Salvation Army, had read the entire Bible through eight times by the age of twelve. Have you read it through even once? And when you read, do you pray for understanding?

Mary Jones was born in 1784 in Wales. Her father told her Bible stories, and she longed to read the Bible. Her family was too poor to buy a Bible, and Mary could not read. A farmer's wife who lived two miles away told Mary that when she learned to read, she could come to their house and read their Bible. When a neighborhood school opened, Mary attended and learned how to read by the age of ten. She then walked the two miles to the neighbor's house to read their Bible and memorized entire chapters at a time. Every Saturday, she walked the two miles just to read the Bible, and for the next six years, Mary saved money by doing jobs for neighbors.

When she was sixteen years old, Mary heard about Pastor Charles in the town of Bala – about twenty-five miles away. He had Bibles for sale. She took her money and walked the twenty-five miles barefoot so she wouldn't ruin her one pair of shoes. When she found the pastor, he told her he had sold most of the Bibles, and the remaining few had been promised to others. The Welsh Bible Society that had printed them had no plans to print more, but when he heard her story, he gave her his last copy, which he had reserved for someone else.

Her story inspired many, and, with the help of Pastor

3   James S. Hewitt, ed., *Illustrations Unlimited*.

Charles, the British and Foreign Bible Society soon formed to help provide more Bibles. Does the Bible mean as much to you as it did to Mary Jones?

A. W. Tozer once said, "The Bible is the easiest book in the world to understand for the spiritual mind, but one of the hardest for the carnal mind." It is very important that we read the Bible not with our own understanding, but through "spiritual eyes."

Prayer

Father, thank you for giving us Your Word – not only the written Word that we call the Bible, but the Word made flesh who dwelt among us and died for us – Jesus Christ Your Son, the Lamb of God. May we not only talk about the Bible, but help us to love, learn, and live your Word. May we take Your Word as our final authority as You continue to change our hearts and conform us to the image of Your Son, Jesus Christ, through the power of Your Holy Spirit.

Help us not to follow religion or make excuses, but to go to You and ask You to open the eyes of our understanding and make sure that what we believe is not the mere doctrine or rules of man, but Your Holy Word. Remind us that if leaders teach things contrary to the Bible, then they are wrong, but Lord, Your Word is true and faithful forever.

Teach us to follow Jesus Christ and to live as He lived, telling others about Him and doing what is right in Your eyes only. May we not fear man, but fear You, not being afraid of any man, as long as we can follow the Alpha and Omega, the Son of God, the King of kings, the head of the Church – Jesus Christ our Lord and Savior, in whose name we pray. Amen.

Chapter 5

THE CHURCH

Ecclesiology

For the husband is the head of the wife, even as Christ is the head of the church: and he is the saviour of the body. (Ephesians 5:23)

Introduction

The Old Testament accounts relating to the worship of God make it clear that by the time Jesus walked this earth, the worship and service of the Jews no longer resembled what God had originally given them hundreds of years earlier. We, too, could be in danger of forgetting what God's purpose for the Church is. Has the church service become just a tradition without real meaning? Something that makes us feel religious, but leaves us empty afterward. In this chapter, we'll take a look at ecclesiology – the doctrine and study of the church. Sadly, churches of every kind, whether "conservative" or "liberal," are today struggling and weak. Compared to what we see in the Scriptures, it appears that churches overall are lukewarm or asleep. It is time to wake up and do the work of the Church – Christ is coming back soon.

What the Amish Teach

What most Anabaptists, both Mennonite and Amish, generally believe is stated for us in the *1632 Dordrecht Confession of Faith*. Of the eighteen articles listed in this *Confession of Faith*, eleven pertain to the church. Of these eleven, nine concern specific practices and ordinances that include baptism, the Holy Supper, foot washing, marriage, relation to secular authority, revenge, oaths, the ban, and shunning. The remaining two are devoted to the "Church of Christ," and the "Election, and Offices of Teachers, Deacons, and Deaconesses, in the Church." The reality is that the articles aren't fully held to today. One case in point is that they speak of the ordination of deaconesses. Most conservative Mennonites and Amish do not practice that today. The following is a short list of Amish church-related terms:

Ausbund: This historic Anabaptist song book, used in most Amish churches, also provides descriptions of Amish teachings.

The Church: That Amish group which has the correct form and practice. Other denominations, the Mennonites, or other Amish groups are viewed as apostate and are not the ideal church.

Church Membership: There is hardly hope of salvation without it. Church membership includes a vow of submission to church rules and leadership. This is marked by submitting to water baptism.

Righteousness: A person who models the church rules and the good things of Scripture, such as being peaceable, not soon angry, etc. is considered righteous. Jesus may finish making a person fully righteous *if* after death that person gets a white robe.

Baptism: The doorway to the church; the point at which all previous sins are washed away.

Ordinances: *Ordnung* is a German word for order, discipline, rule, arrangement, organization, or system. This is a behavioral code, a list of guidelines for daily living, a discipline, and a standard. These are practices such as baptism and the Holy Supper, derived from Scripture, but the *Ordnung* also includes an established letter which spells out practical details, including such things as beards, pleats, brims, electricity, silo roofs, etc.

What the Scriptures Teach

What is the church? It refers to all those who have been baptized by God's Spirit into the body of believers through belief in the gospel of Jesus Christ – immersed into a spiritual body (1 Corinthians 12:13). Has the Church replaced Israel as God's witness on earth? According to Romans 11:11, no: *God forbid: but rather through their fall salvation is come unto the Gentiles, for to provoke them* [the Jews] *to jealousy.*

In the New Testament, we see the word *church* used most often to describe each individual group of like-minded believers in a certain locale. We call them local churches – each one independently governing itself under the Holy Spirit's guidance.

The Beginning of the Church

Up until the resurrection of Jesus Christ, God's focus was on the Jews. They were made up of only one nation, Israel, and they were centered in Jerusalem. Their purpose was to reflect God's image and make Him known to the world in word and lifestyle. *Ye are my witnesses, saith the Lord, and my servant whom I have chosen: that ye may know and believe me, and understand that I am he: before me there was no God formed, neither shall there be after me* (Isaiah 43:10). They preached the coming Messiah who would save them from their enemies and rule over them forever in Jerusalem (Jeremiah 23:5-8). Their hope was in an earthly kingdom.

In the Gospels, we find the Jewish believers overwhelmed with sorrow at Christ's death. Soon after, they were overjoyed by His resurrection. In Acts, we see them confused at Christ's ascension, but rejoicing at Pentecost when they were baptized with the Holy Spirit, who had come to take Jesus' place on earth. While the nation of Israel had its beginning in Abraham, Isaac, and Jacob, the Church began on the day of Pentecost as recorded in Acts 2.

With the Holy Spirit's presence in their lives, the New Testament saints understood their purpose on earth, which was not unlike Israel's purpose – to make God known to the uttermost parts of the world, in word and lifestyle, beginning in Jerusalem. *And that repentance and remission of sins should be preached in his name among all nations, beginning at Jerusalem* (Luke 24:47). We find that the New Testament Church is made up of both Jews *and* Gentiles. The Church's message is that the Messiah came, died, was buried, rose from the dead, and is coming again to gather up the Church to live with Him forever in heaven. The Christian's hope is in a heavenly kingdom (1 Corinthians 15:1-19).

Even though the gospel of Jesus Christ was made known to Abraham so long ago (Galatians 3:8-9), God's will for the Church was only revealed in the New Testament. The apostle Paul wrote it this way: *If ye have heard of the dispensation* [privilege] *of the grace of God which is given me to you-ward: How that by revelation he made known unto me the mystery . . . which in other ages was not made known unto the sons of men, as it is now revealed unto his holy apostles and prophets by the Spirit; That the Gentiles should be fellowheirs and of the same body, and partakers of his promise in Christ by the gospel* (Ephesians 3:2-6).

Galatians 3:26-29 gives a good definition of the Church: *For ye are all the children of God by faith in Christ Jesus. For as many of you as have been baptized* [by the Spirit] *into Christ, have put on Christ*, whether Jew or Gentile, slaves or freemen, men or women, *ye are all one in Christ Jesus. And if ye be Christ's, then are ye Abraham's seed, and heirs according to the promise.* Gentile believers do not become Jews, but are grafted in among them because of their faith in Christ (Romans 11:11-25).

The Head

And [the Father] *hath put all things under* [the Son's] *feet and gave him to be the head over all things to the church* (Ephesians 1:22). A body cannot live without a head. The body needs a head to tell it when to move, when it's hungry, when it's hurting, when it's cold, etc. In any one local church, you will have many members working different jobs, but they need a head to keep everything running smoothly (1 Corinthians 12:12-31). If the foot decided to make the decisions for everyone, all would be stomping and kicking each other. Mankind was not made to function without a head. Christ has been appointed as our authority (our head). He alone has the right to tell us what to do and how to do it.

I remember growing up thinking that my grandparents watched my every move from heaven, as if they were my judges, because of what my dad taught me. Upon studying the Bible, I found I was believing a lie. Yes, my dad taught me a lie! I'm sure he did it innocently, but I learned through that lie that all our instructions concerning the Church and Christian living should come from our Head, Jesus Christ alone.

Do you remember how close God the Son was with His Father? Jesus wanted that same closeness with all those who followed Him in faith. He prayed in John 17:21 *That they all* (the Church) *may be one; as thou, Father, art in me, and I in*

67

thee, that they also may be one in us: that the world may believe that thou hast sent me. Ephesians 5:22-33 uses this close, loving relationship of Christ and His church as an example for marriage. This is the Church's goal: to be so close in relationship to Christ that we forget about our own selfish desires and live to bring glory to our Head. We bring glory to Him by spending time with Him, by obeying His every command under the Holy Spirit's control, and by making Him known to the world, as John the Baptist did in John 1:7. The Church is *for a witness, to bear witness of the Light, that all men through* [the Church] *might believe.*

The Body

Under the Old Testament, Israel had a temple in Jerusalem in which they were commanded to worship, and they will again have a temple in Jerusalem during the one thousand-year reign of Christ when He returns. But, within the New Testament church, each member is a temple, because each person has been baptized by the Holy Spirit. *Know ye not that ye are the temple of God, and that the Spirit of God dwelleth in you?* (1 Corinthians 3:16). Therefore, New Testament believers are allowed to meet together for worship and prayer anywhere (Matthew 18:20). The actual building has nothing to do with it. Matthew 10:25 describes the body (the Church) as Christ's *household*. Other passages describe it as the *salt and light* of the world (Matthew 5:13); Christ's *flock* (Matthew 26:31); a *kingdom*, because Jesus, as King, rules in the hearts of the Church (Matthew 16:19; Romans 8:16-17). And, because the Church is built upon the *rock* [Christ], it will last forever (Matthew 16:18).

Members of the Church are considered *members one of another* (Romans 12:5). No one believer is to be independent of another. Can you imagine one of your ears taking off to live on its own without the rest of the body? That would be silly. It couldn't survive without the body. The work of the Church is a group effort. The Church is not just your local denomination, but includes each and every genuine Christian, of all sorts of denominations and races.

God's Spirit has given each member a spiritual gift for service to God. This does not refer to our human talents we receive at birth, but spiritual talents for the work of the Church that we receive at our second birth. These gifts are *for the perfecting of the saints, for the work of the ministry, for the edifying of the body of Christ* (Ephesians 4:12). No gift is more important than another. In God's eyes, the person who waits tables at a fellowship meal is just as important as the one who preaches. Every member of a local church body who functions in their spiritual gift brings glory to their head, Jesus Christ. Yet without the Spirit's control in our lives, our works would never be considered good, because they would be done in the flesh, in our own strength (Romans 8:1-11).

We need each other, as much as our physical body needs each part in order to function as a whole. Scripture says, *And let us consider one another to provoke unto love and to good works; Not forsaking the assembling of ourselves together, as the manner of some is; but exhorting one another: and so much the more as ye see the day approaching* (Hebrews 10:24-25).

In Acts chapter 7, Stephen delivers a wonderful sermon on the history of God's dealing with the Jewish nation in the wilderness, made up not only of the offspring of Jacob who were delivered out of Egypt, but also of a *mixed multitude* (Exodus 12:37-38). This assembly was made up of both those who had a heart after God and those who were along just because they were born Jews. God's covenant was with the whole nation of Israel. Ponder the fact that twelve spies went into the Promised Land, but only two of them believed God. This ratio of two out of twelve may well represent the nation as a whole.

The Church, however, is made up of only God's children, whom He adopts because of their faith in the Son. They come from every nation on earth. We might find both believers and nonbelievers in any local church gathering. Some of the non-believers may even be "members" of that local church, but God does not recognize unbelievers as members of *His* Church. By faith, the Spirit births us into the Church (1 Corinthians 12:12-13). We should not even think about becoming a member of a local church if we are not yet a member of Christ's Church. The local church is a place where each individual Christian can practice their faith with worship, group prayer, fellowship, and meeting the needs of each other. As you see, God never taught us in His Word that one can receive His grace through church membership. The church cannot save our souls.

Church Ordinances

Many denominations identify members with the local church gathering by water baptism. But, Church members are commanded to be baptized as a testimony of faith in Jesus Christ. Baptism symbolizes the death, burial, and resurrection of Christ. Baptism was never meant to cleanse us from our sin. It is a statement to those who observe that we have already been cleansed by the blood of Christ as a result of faith in His gospel. The Ethiopian in Acts 8:36-39 is a good example of a believer who immediately obeyed the command of baptism after believing the gospel. Sadly, the Roman Catholic Church of the Middle Ages (the state church) taught that baptism, not Christ, was the cleansing agent. They also taught that to become a member of the church, one must make a vow of loyalty to that church. And, if they ever left that church, they lost their hope of salvation. This was the teaching of our forefathers before they left the state church to become Anabaptists, and this false teaching seems to have been overlooked and carried over into the Amish and Mennonite churches. But, as we see in Scripture, this was never taught by Christ or the apostles. Our loyalty must to be toward Jesus Christ and Him alone. To pledge your loyalty to the church is to pledge loyalty to man, not Christ. God asks us to submit to Him, but does not force us. He calls us and woos us to Himself for our own good, but He never gave the church authority to force us to live in a certain way. Yes, He commands us to submit to our church elders, but for our own good, not for the purpose of forcing us to live under a set of manmade rules. The local church is God's tool for our spiritual growth and for getting the gospel out to the world.

Another ordinance of the Church is the Lord's Supper, as taught in 1 Corinthians 11. We don't usually like to think about how our loved ones died, but we are commanded to remember how Christ died. His death was an act of the highest love, and He did it willingly (1 Peter 2:21-25). God knew how forgetful we are (just like the Israelites). We need constant reminders of Christ's shed blood and broken body, which are symbolized by bread (Christ was called the Bread of Life) and the juice of crushed grapes (the pouring out of His blood). Some of us need reminded more often than others. That is why Jesus said to remember Him *as often as ye eat this bread and drink this cup* (1 Corinthians 11:26). There is no limit as to how often a local church can celebrate Christ's death and resurrection, but it should be done regularly. It is a time for repeated examination of our lives to see whether our focus is still on doing the will of God – to examine what sins we've been harboring and whom we have not yet forgiven. The Lord's Supper keeps us serious about sin and eternally grateful to our Savior. It renews our love and commitment to Him and keeps us excited for His return.

Church Order
When traveling around this world, I have seen churches of

every shape and size. Some church services are loud, some are quiet, some treat church as a country club, while others put great importance on ritual. Culture has a lot to do with our methods for worshiping God. God knew we would criticize and judge each other within the Church body, so He gave us some guidelines *and* some liberties. We have to be very careful that our motives for ruling a church are to bring honor to Christ. As head of the Church body, Christ instituted order by instructing us to ordain elders in each local church gathering (1 Timothy and Titus). The goal of church leadership is to unify the body by sound Bible teaching guided by the Holy Spirit; that all believe the same thing about Christ as taught in Scripture; that all grow up into mature sons and daughters of God able to do the work of the Lord without being deceived by false teachers, bringing glory and honor to their Head. *Let the beauty of the LORD our God be upon us* (Psalm 90:17). And, these elders/bishops have the authority from Christ to discipline false teachers and unruly members who seek to glorify themselves.

In the local church, one member, under the Spirit's control, may have liberty to do what another thinks is sin. Take careful consideration to these passages on Christian liberties: Romans 14:1-15:13; 1 Corinthians 8; Colossians 2:16-23.

Missionary Work

One of the great commands to the Church is to go and *teach all nations, baptizing them in the name of the Father, and of the Son, and of the Holy Ghost: Teaching them to observe all things whatsoever I have commanded you* (Matthew 28:19-20). Acts 14:21-23 teaches us how the apostle Paul went about "planting" local churches in areas where Christ was unknown. *And when they* [Paul and company] *had preached the gospel to that city, and had taught many . . .* they had a local church – a group of believers in the gospel of Christ. Paul periodically returned to these areas where he had preached to *confirm* the believers, making sure they understood God's message correctly. He *exhorted,* or strongly urged, them to continue in the faith, because they would be persecuted for following Christ. Then, he would ordain *elders in every church.* The word *ordain* in this passage is said to mean *stretched out the hand.*

Paul continued teaching them in more depth as the Holy Spirit taught him. He was like a shepherd to the converts, training them in the ways of God in order to enjoy what Christ's death, burial, and resurrection offered them, helping them to grow in their spiritual understanding. The results of Paul's concern for the local church are his Spirit-inspired epistles (letters) which he wrote for our instruction, even to this day. The epistles of the apostles in the New Testament are what churches heavily lean on as examples for the local church, although we are commanded to *preach the word* (2 Timothy 4:2) – every word of the Bible. Paul was an example of one who preached the word, as seen in Acts 20:27 where he said, *For I have not shunned to declare unto you all the counsel of God.* Paul was a good example of a loving overseer who cared for the spiritual welfare of his flock and the reputation of Jesus Christ.

Faith Is the Root of the Church

The first chapter of 1 Peter talks to the Church in general – that it is *kept by the power of God through faith unto salvation.* Their *faith* must be tried in order to be strengthened and bring *honor and glory* to Christ at His appearing. Their suffering was only *for a season.* And, even though they can't see their Savior, they can still *rejoice with joy unspeakable,* because they love Him (1 Peter 1:5-8). Let's look at three strengths of the church in 1 Corinthians 13:13, which says: *And now abideth faith, hope, charity, these three; but the greatest of these is charity.*

Each individual member of the church has been given *all*

*things that pertain unto life and godliness, through the **knowledge of him** that hath called us to glory and virtue* (2 Peter 1:3). Faith in Christ is just the beginning, the root, of a Christian's life. God expects our faith to grow and produce fruit – the fruit of the Spirit (Galatians 5:22-23). The Church is to reflect the image of Christ and to get along with each other by bearing spiritual fruit.

In 2 Peter 1, the Church is told to give *all diligence* to ***add to your faith*.** According to verses five through seven, each individual member of the church is to add *virtue* [qualities of excellence], *knowledge, temperance* [self-control of our fleshly desires], *patience, godliness, brotherly kindness,* and *charity.* God desires His Church to be pure – to be a valuable tool through which He can do His will on earth. That means we must cultivate our faith in order to grow. Spiritual cultivation includes Bible study and prayer. The more you do it, the more familiar you will become with God, and in turn, the Spirit will produce His fruit through you.

Hope Is the Purifier of the Church

Empowered by the Holy Spirit, the believers at Pentecost eagerly went to work for their Lord. They pressed on in hope of His promised return (Acts 1:11; John 14:2-3). Peter, in his first letter to the local churches, calls it a *lively hope* – alive because Jesus is alive. 1 John 3:2-3 says that *when* [Jesus] *shall appear, we shall be like him; for we shall see him as he is* [in His glorified body]. *And every man that hath this hope in him purifieth himself, even as he is pure.*

Biblical hope is not to wish for something to happen. It is a sure guarantee – a trusted expectation that Christ will keep His promises. You can't have hope without faith. Pastor and author Jim Andrews says that Eve believed the serpent's lies in the Garden of Eden out of blind faith, not saving faith. It produced no hope, because she had no prior knowledge as to the character of the serpent. She didn't know whether he could be trusted or not, because there was no history of promises kept. This was quite the opposite of Sarah, who believed *because she judged him faithful who had promised* (Hebrews 11:11). And, as it says in verse 6 of the same chapter, *for he that cometh to God must believe that He is* [faith], *and that He is a rewarder of them that **diligently** seek Him* [hope]. The Church cannot be useful to Christ, its head, without knowing and believing Him. The more we get to know Him, the more we will trust Him and find that He does indeed keep His promises. Faith/hope is knowing without a shadow of a doubt that Jesus Christ will do what He said He will do.

Hope motivates the Church to keep their hearts clean because they want to please their Savior and be ready when He comes for them. As *labourers together with God,* the Church is built on the foundation of Christ (1 Corinthians 3:9-15), but they are to *take heed how* they build it – whether they do it in the Spirit (in faith) or in the flesh (in unbelief). Before entering into the new heaven and earth, all believers will have to stand before the judgment seat of Christ. *Every* [saved] *man's work shall be made manifest,* or visible, on that day and will be judged. Notice, the believers' *works* will be judged, not the believer, because their names are already written in the Lamb's Book of Life (1 Corinthians 3:11-15). They will either *receive a reward* or *suffer* the *loss* of a reward for their works, depending on its quality. As the poem by C. T. Studd states, "Only one life, 'twill soon be past. Only what's done for Christ will last."

Christ promised to come back to this earth to lead His body into heaven for the wedding feast. As the groom, Jesus will present the Church to His Father as His perfect bride, made perfect by the blood of Christ (Revelation 19:7-8). The apostle Paul's desire was to do his part in preparing the Church for that hour, saying, *that I may present you as a chaste virgin to Christ* – to avoid as much sin as possible before that day (2 Corinthians 11:2). Christ's return is the hope of the church, and that hope encourages us to be found holy in our thoughts and lifestyle (John 14:1-3; Philippians 3:20-21; Colossians 3:1-4).

Love Is the Brand of the Church

Many of our characteristics show who we are. Our accent tells what part of the country we're from. The way we dress gives clues as to whether we're a doctor, a biker, or Amish. Even cattle are branded in order to identify to whom they belong. If you belong to Christ, can people tell? They won't be able to tell by our outward appearance, but by what comes out of our hearts.

Each child of God should show Christ's brand on their life. Jesus said that the outstanding mannerism of a believer should be the love of God. *By this shall all men know that ye are my disciples, if ye have love one to another* (John 13:35). This is not just a warm feeling. It's a supernatural love that only the Spirit of God can produce in a person of faith, as shown in 1 Corinthians 13.

Being a child of God is a great honor, something the Church should advertise by its thoughts, words, and actions. Christ dearly wants the Church to shine forth His love. God uses His love to unify the brethren and draw others to Christ for salvation. Love for our Savior, not duty, should be the Church's motivation to obey His commands. Will you love the return of Christ, or does the thought of it put fear into your heart? If you have fear, you have no hope.

Conclusion

These three simple phrases, which are posted in many church buildings, can characterize the job of each local church:

EXALT THE SAVIOR – worship Him (putting Jesus Christ first) in song, in teaching, and in fellowship (Ephesians 3:21; 5:19-21).

EDIFY THE SAINTS – *teach no other doctrine* but that which is stated in the Scriptures, heeding *godly edifying which is in faith,* and to love *out of a pure heart, and of a good conscience* with truthful faith (1 Timothy 1:3-5; 2 Timothy 4:2-3).

EVANGELIZE THE LOST – *go ye therefore, and teach all nations, baptizing them in the name of the Father, and of the Son, and of the Holy Ghost; teaching them to observe all things whatsoever I have commanded you* (Matthew 28:19-20; Acts 1:8)

And they continued stedfastly in the apostles' doctrine and fellowship, and in breaking of bread, and in prayers . . . praising God and having favour with all the people. And the Lord added to the church daily such as should be saved (Acts 2:42, 47).

Prayer

Open our eyes, dear Father, to see the beauty of Your holiness and of our utter emptiness. Help us see the vanity of our plans and of our own righteousness. May we experience more fully our completion *in Him.* Thank You for Jesus, who is made unto us righteousness. Make us that one perfect man in Christ. Since our position is already complete *in Him*, we look forward to the completion of Your perfect work when Jesus returns. While we are still here, help us to see more and more of Your wisdom, Your work, and Your great mystery.

In the name of Jesus, Amen.

Chapter 6

ANGELS, DEMONS, AND SATAN

Angelology and Demonology

For by him were all things created, that are in heaven, and that are in earth; visible and invisible, whether they be thrones, or dominions, or principalities, or powers: all things were created by him, and for him. (Colossians 1:16)

Introduction

Most of us grew up knowing that angels, demons, and the devil exist, but what do we know about them? Usually, our churches taught very little about the extent of their power or the function of the spirit. No one talked much about angels. The term *Holy Ghost*, rather than the term *Holy Spirit*, was the most commonly used, which gave many of us a spooky concept of the spirit world. Throughout history, an absence of biblical knowledge has often resulted in superstition filling the void. The word *spirit* simply means *a supernatural being without a flesh-and-blood body.* Scripture shows us that these spirits are typically invisible, though they may appear in visible form or even as men.

On the other hand, we were taught much about Satan and

his desire to lead us astray from God. The blame for many of our sinful actions was attributed to him. Satan and hell went hand in hand and instilled much fear in us. Threats to make us behave often tapped into this fear.

There are a variety of false teachings about the spirit world – some that can raise your hair. By diligent study of God's Word, though, we can understand why God created these invisible creatures, their purpose and involvement in our lives, and whether we should fear them or not.

What the Amish Teach

We find these few comments on the subject of angels and demons in the *Dordrecht Confession of Faith*:

> "He [God] is the Creator of all things visible and *invisible*." (Article 1)

> Adam and Eve were "seduced by the subtlety and deceit of the serpent, and the envy of the *devil*." (Article 2)

> "… nor through *angels* . . . could [they] be raised." (Article 2)

> ". . . destroyed the works of the *devil*. . . ." (Article 4)

> "God . . . will dwell and walk among them, and preserve them, so that no floods or tempests, nay, not even the gates of *hell,* shall move or prevail against them." (Article 8)

The subject is touched upon in parts of *In Meiner Jugend* (an Amish devotional book), under Rules of a Godly Life. We read in Part 1:

> "Think often on . . . *hell,* for there is nothing more unbearable." (No. 3)

"Likewise, even the smallest sin, if it is cherished and not repented of, can bring a man down to *hell.*" (No. 11)

"The way to *hell* is always full of wandering souls. . . . God would say, 'Because you have sinned with the majority, you must also be cast into *hell* with the majority.'" (No. 14)

Then in Part 3 we find:

"*Satan* can possess your soul and keep it in his control by means of a single sin." (No. 2)

"Avoid idleness as a resting-pillow of the *devil* . . . . Great is the power the *devil* has over the slothful." (No. 10)

"No sin was punished more severely than pride. It changed *angels* into *devils.*" (No. 11)

One of the prayers of *In Meiner Jugend* touches upon the subject:

"Let me not be an instrument of the *evil spirit* lest he exercise and fulfill his wickedness . . . through me. For such is the image of *Satan.*" (page 111)

Later in this same document, candidates for baptism are asked to "renounce the *devil*" (page 195). From all of these passages, we gained a fear and a ready awareness of the presence of evil spirits.

What the Scriptures Teach

Who Are These Invisible Spirits?
As Colossians 1:16 states, God created the *invisible* world – the spirit world. The Bible commonly calls beings from this realm

angels, yet God has many other names for them: cherubim, seraphim, messengers, hosts of the Lord or of heaven, ministers, powers, principalities, stars or morning stars, rulers in high places, and sons of God. Some are referred to by specific names: *Lucifer* (Isaiah 14:12), *Gabriel* (Daniel 9:21; Luke 1:19), and *Michael* (Jude 9). Others are simply referred to in a general sense as those who ruled over other angels, too numerous for us to count (Revelation 5:11).

We know the angels were in existence before God created the earth because when God *laid the foundations of the earth . . . the morning stars sang together, and all the sons of God shouted for joy* (Job 38:4, 7). They were created as holy, eternal creatures (they don't die).

We know angels are mighty in strength. David wrote: *Bless the LORD, ye his angels, that excel in strength, that do his commandments, hearkening unto the voice of his word* (Psalm 103:20).

Jesus told us that angels do not marry, *For when they* [men] *shall rise from the dead, they neither marry, nor are given in marriage; but are as the angels which are in heaven* (Mark 12:25). We humans were made *a little lower than the angels,* and the human side of Jesus was also made *a little lower than the angels,* so He would be able to die (Psalm 8:5; Hebrews 2:9). Yet, as the Son of God, He was *so much better than the angels,* and *all the angels of God* were urged to *worship Him* (Hebrews 1:4, 6). Christ has authority over them, because He created them, *which from the beginning of the world hath been hid in God, who created all things by Jesus Christ* (Ephesians 3:9). Even though the angels are higher, mightier, and wiser than we are, we must never give our worship to them. *Let no man beguile you of your reward in a voluntary humility and worshipping of angels*, but we can thank the Lord for them (Colossians 2:18).

What Is Their Purpose?

Angels were created as *ministering* [serving] *spirits, sent forth to minister* [to believers in Christ] (Hebrews 1:14). What a comforting thought to know that God sends out His angels to help us in our weakness and ignorance. Throughout the Bible, we read many instances of angels coming to earth to attend to God's people or to deliver messages to them:

An angel ministered to Elijah in the wilderness.

> *And as he lay and slept under a juniper tree, behold, then an angel touched him, and said unto him, Arise and eat.*
>
> *And he looked, and, behold, there was a cake baken on the coals, and a cruse of water at his head. And he did eat and drink, and laid him down again.*
>
> *And the angel of the LORD came again the second time, and touched him, and said, Arise and eat; because the journey is too great for thee* (1 Kings 19:5-7).

The beggar Lazarus *died, and was carried by the angels into Abraham's bosom* (Luke 16:22).

Later, Peter was put in prison by Herod and heavily guarded.

> *And behold, the angel of the Lord came upon him, and a light shined in the prison: and he smote Peter on the side, and raised him up, saying, arise up quickly. And his chains fell off from his hands.*
>
> *And the angel said unto him, Gird* [prepare or equip] *thyself, and bind on thy sandals. And so he did. And he saith unto him Cast thy garment about thee, and follow me.*

And he went out, and followed him; and wist not that it was true which was done by the angel; but thought he saw a vision.

When they were past the first and the second ward, they came unto the iron gate that leadeth unto the city; which opened to them of his own accord: and they went out, and passed on through one street; and forthwith the angel departed from him.

And when Peter was come to himself, he said, Now I know of a surety, that the Lord hath sent his angel, and hath delivered me out of the hand of Herod, and from all the expectation of the people of the Jews (Acts 12:7-11).

In Genesis, Hagar fled when Sarai treated her harshly.

And an angel of the LORD found her by a fountain of water in the wilderness, by the fountain in the way to Shur.

And he said, Hagar, Sarai's maid, whence camest thou? And whither wilt thou go? And she said, I flee from the face of my mistress Sarai.

And the angel of the LORD said unto her, Return to thy mistress, and submit thyself under her hands.

And the angel of the LORD said unto her, I will multiply thy seed exceedingly, that it shall not be numbered for multitude.

And the angel of the LORD said unto her, Behold, thou art with child, and shalt bear a son, and shalt call his name Ishmael; because the LORD hath heard thy affliction (Genesis 16:7-11).

In Jerusalem was a pool called Bethesda where many ailing people gathered.

> *For an angel went down at a certain season into the pool, and troubled the water: whosoever then first after the troubling of the water stepped in was made whole of whatsoever disease he had* (John 5:4).

After Jesus had been in the tomb for three days,

> *there was a great earthquake: for the angel of the Lord descended from heaven, and came and rolled back the stone from the door, and sat upon it. His countenance was like lightning, and his raiment white as snow: And for fear of him the keepers did shake, and became as dead men. And the angel answered and said unto the women, Fear not ye: for I know that ye seek Jesus, which was crucified* (Matthew 28:2-5).

An angel even spoke through Balaam's donkey:

> *And God's anger was kindled because he [Balaam] went: and the angel of the LORD stood in the way for an adversary against him. Now he was riding upon his ass, and his two servants were with him.*

> *And the ass saw the angel of the LORD standing in the way, and his sword drawn in his hand: and the ass turned aside out of the way, and went into the field: and Balaam smote the ass, to turn her into the way.*

> *But the angel of the LORD stood in a path of the vineyards, a wall being on this side, and a wall on that side. And when the ass saw the angel of the LORD, she thrust herself unto the wall, and crushed*

Balaam's foot against the wall: and he smote her again.

And the angel of the LORD went further, and stood in a narrow place, where was no way to turn either to the right hand or to the left. And when the ass saw the angel of the LORD, she fell down under Balaam: and Balaam's anger was kindled, and he smote the ass with a staff.

And the Lord opened the mouth of the ass, and she said unto Balaam, What have I done unto thee, that thou hast smitten me these three times?

And Balaam said unto the ass, Because thou hast mocked me: I would there were a sword in mine hand, for now would I kill thee.

And the ass said unto Balaam, Am not I thine ass, upon which thou hast ridden ever since I was thine unto this day? was I ever wont to do so unto thee? and he said, Nay.

Then the LORD opened the eyes of Balaam, and he saw the angel of the LORD standing in the way, and his sword drawn in his hand: and he bowed down his head, and fell flat on his face (Numbers 22:22-31).

God used angels to announce his great plan of salvation to Abraham, Zacharias, and Mary and Joseph, but the list of angels' involvement with humans in history could fill a book of its own. Angels do God's will in heaven as well as on earth, and God still uses them in our lives.

The Bible tells us that God gave his angels the job of protecting us. *For he shall give his angels charge over thee, to keep thee in all thy ways. They shall bear thee up in their hands, lest thou dash thy foot against a stone* (Psalm 91:11-12). In this way, God protected Daniel in the lions' den, and Daniel proclaimed, *My God hath sent his angel, and hath shut the lions' mouths, that they have not hurt me* (Daniel 6:22). In Psalm 34:7, David tells us that *the angel of the LORD encampeth round about them that fear him, and delivereth them.*

How comforting that even our little children who haven't yet come to faith in Christ are watched over by angels. Jesus told those who were following Him to *take heed that ye despise not one of these little ones; for I say unto you, That in heaven their angels do always behold the face of my Father which is in heaven* (Matthew 18:10). When they do come to accept Christ as their Savior, the heavenly Father and His angels rejoice together as they do for every sinner who repents. Jesus said: *I say unto you, that likewise joy shall be in heaven over one sinner that repenteth, more than over ninety and nine just persons, which need no repentance. . . . There is joy in the presence of the angels of God over one sinner that repenteth* (Luke 15:7, 10).

The angels observe us, watching God's every move on earth in amazement of His grace and mercy, and probably in disbelief at our rebellion towards God. Paul wrote to the Ephesians about this:

> *And to make all men see what is the fellowship of the mystery, which from the beginning of the world hath been hid in God, who created all things by Jesus Christ: To the intent that now unto the principalities and powers in heavenly places might be known by the church the manifold wisdom of God, according to the eternal purpose which he purposed in Christ Jesus our Lord.* (Ephesians 3:9-11)

Another task given to angels is one of delivering judgment on those who reject God on earth. For instance, *the angel of the Lord smote* [Herod], *because he gave not God the glory* (Acts 12:23). There are many examples where angels were used to destroy human lives because of their open rebellion against God's grace. After David had numbered the people, God used an angel to bring judgment. *And when the angel stretched out his hand upon Jerusalem to destroy it, the Lord repented him of the evil, and said to the angel that destroyed the people, It is enough* (2 Samuel 24:16).

In 2 Kings 19:35, we read that *the angel of the LORD went out, and smote in the camp of the Assyrians an hundred fourscore and five thousand: and when they arose early in the morning, behold, they were all dead corpses.* Even in the end times we see that God will use angels. John said: *And I heard a great voice out of the temple saying to the seven angels, Go your ways, and pour out the vials of the wrath of God upon the earth* (Revelation 16:1).

Who Are the Devil and His Demons?

The devil's name was originally Lucifer, the *anointed cherub* created in perfection whose *heart was lifted up because of* [his] *beauty* (Ezekiel 28:14, 17). In his pride and conceit, he vowed he would become *like the most High.* The Almighty gave His angels great strength, but how could one of His created beings ever think he could become like his Creator? Yet in Isaiah we read that Lucifer said, *I will ascend into heaven, I will exalt my throne above the stars of God: I will sit also upon the mount of the congregation, in the sides of the north: I will ascend above the heights of the clouds; I will be like the most High* (Isaiah 14:13-14).

God will not tolerate anything contrary to His character. He is perfect. No one can improve upon His might, wisdom, or beauty. Anything inferior to His perfection must be removed from His presence. Lucifer chose to serve himself, for which he was cast out of God's dwelling place. In Isaiah, the Lord declared: *Yet thou shalt be brought down to hell, to the sides of the pit* (Isaiah 14:15). Jesus explained that when the time comes, Satan will be cast into the place of torment prepared for *the devil and his angels* (Matthew 25:41). Satan greatly underestimated God and His Word.

After he rebelled, *Lucifer*, whose name means *the shining one* or *the star of the morning*, became Satan, the adversary, the enemy. He is also called the devil. The angels who followed him in his rebellion became known as demons. They are allowed by God to roam this earth until the time of their eternal punishment. Yet some are being held in captivity until the judgment day because of their gross sin. Second Peter 2:4 says: *God spared not the angels that sinned, but cast them down to hell, and delivered them into chains of darkness, to be reserved unto judgment.* Jude wrote: *And the angels which kept not their first estate, but left their own habitation, he hath reserved in everlasting chains under darkness unto the judgment of the great day* (Jude 6).

These demons have the ability to possess and control a man as they did in the country of the Gadarenes: *there met him* [Jesus] *out of the tombs a man with an unclean spirit, Who had his dwelling among the tombs; and no man could bind him, no, not with chains . . . . And always, night and day, he was in the mountains, and in the tombs, crying, and cutting himself with stones* (Mark 5:2-3, 5). This poor man was tormented by demons, but Jesus cast these unclean spirits out and sent them into a herd of swine. Later, Jesus reminded His disciples that in His *name shall they cast out devils* (Mark 16:17).

When we consider the whole of Scripture, we see that demons cannot dwell together with the Holy Spirit within a true believer. For instance, 2 Corinthians 6:15-16 tells us that Christ and the devil cannot dwell together. For when we become believers, we become the *temple of the living God; as God said,*

"I will dwell in them and walk in them; and I will be their God, and they shall be My people."

Satan has become the god of our world's system. *The god of this world hath blinded the minds of them which believe not, lest the light of the glorious gospel of Christ, who is the image of God, should shine unto them* (2 Corinthians 4:4). The once *shining one* now seeks to put out the light of the One who is our source of light. He entered our world like a rapidly-growing cancer, deceiving his way into the life of Eve, which spread to Adam, and to every generation born after him.

Now the serpent was more subtil [sly] *than any beast of the field which the LORD God had made. And he said unto the woman, Yea, hath God said, Ye shall not eat of every tree of the garden?*

And the woman said unto the serpent, We may eat of the fruit of the trees of the garden: but of the fruit of the tree which is in the midst of the garden, God hath said, Ye shall not eat of it, neither shall ye touch it, lest ye die.

And the serpent said unto the woman, Ye shall not surely die: for God doth know that in the day ye eat thereof, then your eyes shall be opened, and ye shall be as gods, knowing good and evil.

And when the woman saw that the tree was good for food, and that it was pleasant to the eyes, and a tree to be desired to make one wise, she took of the fruit thereof, and did eat, and gave also unto her husband with her; and he did eat. (Genesis 3:1-6)

Satan is effective with his talent for deception, and most of the human race has chosen to worship him, the creature, rather than

God, the Creator. Romans 1:21-25 reveals the progression of evil into our world because of Satan's influence and our unbelief:

> *When they knew God, they glorified him not as God, neither were thankful; but became vain in their imaginations, and their foolish heart was darkened. Professing themselves to be wise, they became fools, and changed the glory of the uncorruptible God into an image made like to corruptible man, and to birds and fourfooted beasts, and creeping things.*
>
> *Wherefore God also gave them up to uncleanness through the lusts of their own hearts, to dishonor their own bodies between themselves: Who changed the truth of God into a lie, and worshipped and served the creature more than the Creator, who is blessed for ever.*

Satan is the father of lies, as Jesus stated: *Ye are of your father the devil, and the lusts of your father ye will do. He was a murderer from the beginning, and abode not in the truth, because there is no truth in him. When he speaketh a lie, he speaketh of his own: for he is a liar, and the father of it* (John 8:44).

Satan refuses to believe that he was defeated at the cross and that we were set free from his hold, but we know *there is therefore now no condemnation to them which are in Christ Jesus, who walk not after the flesh, but after the Spirit. For the law of the Spirit of life in Christ Jesus hath made me free from the law of sin and death* (Romans 8:1-2). Yet he continues his assault on us. We must remember that he *is* a defeated enemy and will leave this world in shame, spending eternity in torment, but not alone. He will take with him those he has infected with rebellion against God. *And the devil that deceived them was cast into the lake of fire and brimstone, where the beast and the false prophet are, and shall be tormented day and night for ever and ever. . . . And whosoever was not found written in the book of life was cast into the lake of fire* (Revelation 20:10, 15).

Casting Out Evil Spirits

> *Howbeit this kind goeth not out but by prayer and fasting.* (Matthew 17:21)

When Jesus sent the twelve apostles on their first mission, He gave them power and authority over demons and diseases. Both the healing of sickness and casting out of demons served as signs that the kingdom of God had come. When seventy others were sent out as recorded in Luke, they also had power over demons. *The seventy returned again with joy, saying, Lord, even the devils are subject unto us through thy name* (Luke 10:17). After Jesus ascended into heaven and established the Church through the coming of the Holy Spirit, we see that people in the days of the early church were healed of sickness and unclean spirits. *There came also a multitude out of the cities round about unto Jerusalem, bringing sick folks, and them which were vexed with unclean spirits: and they were healed every one* (Acts 5:16).

It is God who grants believers power and authority over demons. When Jesus, Peter, James, and John came down from the Mount of Transfiguration, they were greeted by a multitude of people. From among them, a father came up to Jesus and pleaded for Him to heal his son. He had brought the boy to the disciples, but they were unable to heal him. This raises the question: If they had the power and authority to heal, why couldn't they? This is a valid question and one the disciples asked Jesus.

The answer is found in Matthew 17:17 when Jesus called them a *faithless and perverse generation,* and in verse 20, He said it was *because of your unbelief.* Their inability was due to a lack of faith in Christ, not a lack of power or authority. Jesus went on to offer a solution to this lack of faith, saying, *This kind goeth not out but by prayer and fasting* (Matthew 17:21). Prayer and fasting aren't some sort of magical step that gives us power. Instead, they are spiritual disciplines that get our eyes off ourselves and draw us nearer to God and to all He is, which increases our faith in Him. God does not give His power to the faithless, and He chooses when and where to grant that authority and power.

> *When the unclean spirit is gone out of a man, he walketh through dry places, seeking rest; and finding none, he saith, I will return unto my house whence I came out. And when he cometh, he findeth it swept and garnished. Then goeth he, and taketh to him seven other spirits more wicked than himself; and they enter in, and dwell there: and the last state of that man is worse than the first.* (Luke 11:24-26)

When an unclean spirit departs from a person, it leaves behind a vacancy (emptiness). In some cases, the person may try to amend his life on his own. This "cleaning up" or turning over a new leaf, when accomplished by our own determination, is only temporary. We may be prompted to change ourselves by religion, pressure to conform, pleasing others, or ridding ourselves of the consequences of our bad behavior. In this way, the house may be put in order, but it is uninhabited – empty. In Luke, the evil spirit says, *I will return unto **my** house.* The demon couldn't find another place to live, and so decided to go back where it had been. It found the house in order and went and gathered seven other unclean spirits which also entered that man, making his state worse than it was before.

In contrast, God's desire is to fill that vacancy in our heart with His Holy Spirit. When we believe in Jesus and His death, burial, and resurrection, the Holy Spirit comes to live inside us.

First John 4:3-4 says: *And every spirit that confesseth not that Jesus Christ is come in the flesh is not of God*, but for those who are children of God, *greater is he* [the Spirit of God] *that is in you than he that is in the world.* When the Holy Spirit moves into your life, you don't have to fear the evil ones, because you are able to overcome them by God's power (1 John 2:14; Ephesians 6:10-13).

Once we are saved, it doesn't mean we will be sinless. Sometimes we sin through our actions, sometimes by our motives, and often because of what we fail to do. Sin breaks our fellowship with God. As His children, we know that God is ready to forgive us, and we need to turn to Him immediately. *If we confess our sins, he is faithful and just to forgive us our sins, and to cleanse us from all unrighteousness* (1 John 1:9). Unfortunately, human tendency is to not recognize sin for what it is, instead harboring sin in our heart while accusing others of the same things we are guilty of. But, by the power of the Holy Spirit who resides in us, God wants to help us avoid sin in the future. We are to *walk in the Spirit, and ye shall not fulfil the lust of the flesh*, but will grow and mature in the Lord (Galatians 5:16).

What Is God's Purpose in Allowing the Devil and the Demons to Live?

We all ask, "Why didn't God send the devil and his demons to the lake of fire immediately after their rebellion?" Believe it or not, God uses Satan as a part of His plan. Paul told the Corinthians: *And lest I should be exalted above measure through the abundance of the revelations, there was given to me a thorn in the flesh, the messenger of Satan to buffet me, lest I should be exalted above measure* (2 Corinthians 12:7). Paul knew he could easily be proud of his knowledge of the Lord, but this thorn kept him humble.

As the opening verse of this chapter says, *All things were created by him, and for him.* He forms light, and He creates darkness. He makes peace and also creates evil (Isaiah 45:7). He created the angels who rebelled and uses them in His great and mighty plan. God has a purpose for everything – peace for those who trust Him and evil for those who reject Him.

Think about this for a moment: if Satan and his demons had been imprisoned immediately, how would our faith and loyalty to God be tested? How would we grow without trials? How would our character develop without conflict? Remember Job? God allowed Satan to torment Job, but Job refused to curse God. *Naked came I out of my mother's womb, and naked shall I return thither: the LORD gave, and the LORD hath taken away; blessed be the name of the LORD. In all this Job sinned not, nor charged God foolishly* (Job 1:21-22).

How would we know the greatness of God's love, mercy, and truth, if we didn't have the contrast of Satan's hate, injustice, and lies? God, in His all-knowing ways, allows the evil ones to torment and tempt us and spread their lies to us. Even Jesus was allowed to be touched by Satan's hand through persecution, through temptation, and through death.

As we consider God's use of Satan in the life of Job, we see the *sons of God* [angels] *came to present themselves before the LORD, and Satan came also among them* (Job 1:6). When we read the first two chapters of Job, we see that God is the one in charge. He is the one who allowed Satan to use his destructive hand on Job. He gave Satan the power to destroy. God lifted His hedge of protection from around Job and put limits on what Satan could do. We must remember that Satan, even though he is described as *a roaring lion . . . seeking whom he may devour* (1 Peter 5:8), cannot touch us without God's permission. In Job chapters 38 to 42, we see that the Almighty really knows what He is doing when He allows evil to inflict our lives. When an evil one is allowed to use his influence in our lives, it is for a good purpose, for *we know that all things work together for good to them that love God, to them who are the called* [to salvation] *according to His purpose* (Romans 8:28). God desires obedience, and when we fail to obey Him, we must be prodded with painful experiences to get where He wants us to be, for He knows that *godly sorrow worketh repentance* (2 Corinthians 7:10).

Don't forget, the evil ones are created beings. They don't have God's unlimited power to be in all places at once. They are limited to only one location at a time. That is why Satan is constantly *going to and fro in the earth* (Job 1:7). Evil spirits don't have all knowledge as God does. They cannot read our minds, but by observing our actions, they can see where our interests and weaknesses lie and seek to pull us further into sin. They are crafty, sneaky, and very clever in their ways to keep us from worshiping the true and living God of the universe. They constantly try to influence our minds with their lies. That's why God urges us to guard our minds. *Let the words of my mouth, and the meditation of my heart, be acceptable in thy sight, O LORD, my strength, and my redeemer* (Psalm 19:14).

In his letter to the Philippians, Paul said: *Finally, brethren, whatsoever things are true, whatsoever things are honest, whatsoever things are just, whatsoever things are pure, whatsoever things are lovely, whatsoever things are of good report; if there be any virtue, and if there be any praise, think on these things. Those things, which ye have both learned, and received, and heard, and seen in me, do: and the God of peace shall be with you* (Philippians 4:8-9).

Satan will do anything and use anyone to gain our love, loyalty, and obedience. It seems Satan's most common method for drawing us into his hold is to imitate Christ by forming false religions to pull in the masses. The apostle Paul, in a sermon to the immature church at Corinth, stated: *For Satan himself is transformed into an angel of light. Therefore it is no great thing if his ministers* [demons] *also be transformed as the ministers of righteousness; whose end* [judgment] *shall be according to their works* (2 Corinthians 11:14-15). It is *our* works that destroy us. It is the Savior's work that saves us. God warns us again through Paul in Colossians about Satan's type of religion – a religion of human works that makes us feel worthy of God's grace. *Beware lest any man spoil you through philosophy and vain deceit, after the tradition of men, after the rudiments of the world, and not after Christ* (Colossians 2:8).

The evil spirits trick us into worshiping anything other than God Almighty. An idol is anything we deem as more important or more valuable than what God has told us – our personal belongings, our church teachings, our ancestors' ways, or even our parents' advice. If we pledge our loyalty to them before our loyalty to Christ, it is evil, for there are only two roads in life: God's and man's. *No servant can serve two masters: for either he will hate the one, and love the other; or else he will hold to the one, and despise the other* (Luke 16:13). Man's road is Satan's road, for he is our heavenly father unless we turn to the true heavenly Father.

Getting to know God through His Word is the most important thing we can do in our lifetime. Without a good knowledge of the Bible, we might blindly follow Satan, and we won't even realize it is happening. A. W. Tozer once said, "No religion can rise higher than its concept of God." By putting other things or people above our relationship with God, we will only have a cheap religion that is not God's.

From what we read in Scripture, we see that Satan attracts people into his world by offering them power, just as he dared to do with Christ:

And the devil said unto him, All this power will I

*give thee, and the glory of them: for that is delivered
unto me; and to whomsoever I will I give it. If thou
therefore wilt worship me, all shall be thine.*

*And Jesus answered and said unto him, Get thee
behind me, Satan: for it is written, Thou shalt worship the Lord thy God, and him only shalt thou
serve.* (Luke 4:6-8)

Once pulled in by the experience of Satan's powers, a person
will only want more and more. Others may think they are under
a curse from which they cannot escape. It is true that angels,
whether good or evil, *are greater in power and might* than we
are (2 Peter 2:11), but angels and demons are always subject to
the name of Jesus Christ (Ephesians 1:21).

People influenced or possessed by evil spirits often suffer
mental problems, have obsessions with sex or greed, or try to
destroy themselves and others. They become violently angry or
have a strong disrespect toward authority. They also battle with
guilty minds and unreasonable fears. We must not underesti-
mate an evil spirit's power to convince us, as he did Eve, that
practicing sin will bring us greater knowledge and freedom.

Many people are convinced that they have committed the
unpardonable sin by dabbling with the devil. They read of
instances in the Bible of God's refusal to pardon Manasseh for
shedding much innocent blood, but it was the heart of Manasseh
that God judged. His murderous ways were evidence of his
rejection of God. *Manasseh shed innocent blood very much, till
he had filled Jerusalem from one end to another; beside his sin
wherewith he made Judah to sin, in doing that which was evil
in the sight of the LORD* (2 Kings 21:16).

Matthew 12:31-32 speaks of the Pharisees who resisted
Christ much, and even attributed Christ's power as Satan's.
Jesus' answer is sometimes misunderstood, and some become

fearful and uncertain: *Wherefore I say unto you, All manner of sin and blasphemy* [denying, cursing] *shall be forgiven unto men: but the blasphemy against the Holy Ghost shall not be forgiven unto men. And whosoever speaketh a word against the Son of man, it shall be forgiven him: but whosoever speaketh against the Holy Ghost, it shall not be forgiven him, neither in this world, neither in the world to come.* Jesus makes it very clear in Matthew 12 how we will know on which side we are. *He that is not with me is against me; and he that gathereth not with me scattereth abroad* (Matthew 12:30). Do not worry about whether or not some past sin will keep you from heaven, and do not let Satan's lies discourage you. If your heart is still towards the Lord and not against him, you likely have nothing to fear. Focus on *gathering* with Jesus, and let the Holy Spirit lead you into all good things.

Our suffering and torment at the hands of evil spirits may be God's method of turning us from sin. If we respond with a contrite and repentant heart, He is then able to forgive, comfort, strengthen, love, and impart wisdom to us. God will never give the believer in Christ more trials than he is able to handle, and He will always provide a way of escape. *There hath no temptation taken you but such as is common to man: but God is faithful, who will not suffer you to be tempted above that ye are able; but will with the temptation also make a way to escape, that ye may be able to bear it* (1 Corinthians 10:13).

How Can We Guard Ourselves Against Satan and His Evil Spirits?

The gospel of Christ is the only power we have against Satan's domain, *for it is the power of God unto salvation to every one that believeth; to the Jew first, and also to the Greek* (Romans 1:16). The only way to avoid Satan's possession of us is to admit our rebellion toward God and accept Christ's work on the cross as our only method of salvation from sin, Satan, and eternal hell. This one act of total surrender allows the Holy Spirit to possess us, change us, and protect us. This does not mean that the evil spirits will leave us alone, but it makes it impossible for them to enter our body to control it. The demons will continue to harass our minds, but we can even be delivered from that.

As Erwin Lutzer says in his book *God's Devil*, we need:

FAITH in the blood of Christ for salvation: *Being justified freely by his grace through the redemption that is in Christ Jesus: Whom God hath set forth to be a propitiation through faith in his blood* (Romans 3:24-25).

REPENTANCE from sin: *The sacrifices of God are a broken spirit: a broken and a contrite heart, O God, thou wilt not despise* (Psalm 51:17).

TO BE FILLED WITH THE HOLY SPIRIT as a continual surrender to His will: *And be not drunk with wine, wherein is excess; but be filled with the Spirit; Speaking to yourselves in psalms and hymns and spiritual songs, singing and making melody in your heart to the Lord* (Ephesians 5:18-19).

TO BELIEVE GOD'S PROMISES FOR CHRISTIANS: *Nevertheless we, according to his promise, look for new heavens and a new earth, wherein dwelleth righteousness* (2 Peter 3:13).

Our real battles take place in the invisible world, not with our fellow man, *for we wrestle not against flesh and blood, but against principalities, against powers, against the rulers of the darkness of this world, against spiritual wickedness in high places* (Ephesians 6:12). But *if God be for us, who can be against us?* (Romans 8:31), *because greater is He that is in you, than he that is in the world* (1 John 4:4). Believers in Christ have no reason to fear *them which kill the body, but are not able to kill the soul* (Matthew 10:28). Set yourself apart from evil and let God *be your fear, and let him be your dread* (Isaiah 8:13).

Strive to bring glory to the name of God. He wants to be your sanctuary, your room of safety. Run to the arms of the loving Father whenever you sense a demon assaulting you. Call for Him to rebuke the evil ones and trust His promises. If you don't know what those promises are, make an effort to read your Bible over and over and memorize those promises.

Prayer

Dear Heavenly Father, Savior of my soul, deliver me from the evil spirits who seek to bring shame to Your name through me. Please place Your hedge of protection around me. Fill me with Your Spirit that I might not sin against You. Thank you for Your forgiveness. Thank You for the power to turn from sin. Thank You for Your promises to guide and protect me. Help me to die to self-confidence and deliver me from fear. *For I am crucified with Christ. Nevertheless I live, yet not I, but Christ liveth in me. And the life which I now live in the flesh I live by the faith of the Son of God, who loved me, and gave himself for me* (Galatians 2:20). I pray this in the name of Jesus Christ. Amen.

Chapter 7

HUMANITY

Anthropology

And the LORD God formed man of the dust of the ground, and breathed into his nostrils the breath of life; and man became a living soul. (Genesis 2:7)

Introduction

Where did we come from? Why are we here? What is the purpose of life? These questions have occupied the minds of all human beings throughout history. An elderly man once said to me, "See all these books I have?" Bookshelves filled one whole wall of the room from floor to ceiling. He owned books on every religion, books about man's view of life, and books from men who have travelled the world. He said, "I have read every one of these books, searching for the purpose of life, yet I have not found it."

One book in the center of all the others was the Bible – the Holy Scriptures, written by the Creator of the world. When I asked him, the man confessed that he had not yet read that book.

How astonishing! It was the only book on his shelves that held the answers he looked for, but he had no interest in what the all-knowing God had to say.

Our Anabaptist ancestors were interested in going to the Source of life for their answers. They were willing to die for reading and studying a book forbidden to the common man by the state church, for fear that they might find the truth that contradicted church tradition. They might not have understood the Bible well, because it was new to them, but they studied it fervently and understood who they were and what their purpose was on earth.

What the Amish Teach

Article 1 of the Dordrecht Confession of Faith

"Of this same one God, who worketh all in all, we believe and confess that He is the Creator of all things visible and invisible, who in six days created, made, and prepared heaven and earth and sea and all that in them is; and that He still governs and upholds the same and all His works through His wisdom, might, and the word of His power.

"And when He had finished His works, and had ordained and prepared them, each in its nature and properties, good and upright, according to His pleasure, He created the first man, the father of us all, Adam; whom He formed of the dust of the ground, and breathed into his nostrils the breath of life, so that he became a living soul, created by God in His own image and likeness, in righteousness and holiness, unto eternal life. He regarded him above all other creatures, endowed him with many high and glorious gifts, placed him in the pleasure garden or Paradise, and gave him a command and prohibition; afterwards He took a rib from Adam, made a woman therefrom, and brought her to him, joining and giving her to him for a helpmate, companion, and wife; and in consequence of this He also caused, that from this first man Adam, all men that dwell upon the whole earth have descended.

On marriage: "We confess that there is in the church of God an honorable state of matrimony, of two free, believing persons, in accordance with the manner after which God originally ordained the same in Paradise, and instituted it Himself with Adam and Eve, and that the Lord Christ did away and set aside all the abuses of marriage which had meanwhile crept in, and referred all to the original order, and thus left it.

"In this manner the Apostle Paul also taught and permitted matrimony in the church, and left it free for every one to be married, according to the original order, in the Lord, to whomsoever one may get to consent. By these words, in the Lord, there is to be understood, we think, that even as the patriarchs had to marry among their kindred or generation, so the believers of the New Testament have likewise no other liberty than to marry among the chosen generation and spiritual kindred of Christ, namely, such, and no others, who have previously become united with the church as one heart and soul, have received one baptism, and stand in one communion, faith, doctrine and practice, before they may unite with one another by marriage. Such are then joined by God in His church according to the original order; and this is called, marrying in the Lord."

What the Scriptures Teach

Marriage

In the beginning God created the heaven and earth (Genesis 1:1). Since God was the only one present at the beginning of time, He is the only one able to tell us who we are, where we came from, and why we are here. Scripture tells us that God created the heaven and earth for His own pleasure (Revelation 4:11). He *formed the earth . . . to be inhabited* by His special creation, *the children of men* (Isaiah 45:18; Psalm 115:16). He gave man dominion over the earth as a steward, to care for and to have authority over it (Genesis 1:26).

God fashioned Adam and Eve differently from the rest of His creation. He *made* [man] *a little lower than the angels, and hast crowned him with glory and honour* (Psalm 8:5). They were lower because they had bodies like the animals of flesh and blood, covered in skin; but they were higher than the animals, because they were made in His likeness. *God created man in his own image . . . male and female created he them* (Genesis 1:27). God is spirit and has no physical body (John 4:24). God's spiritual image speaks of Adam and Eve's inner self. He made them moral, spiritual beings housed in a physical body. They were a reflection of God Himself. That does not imply that they *were* God. A reflection is never the real thing.

Even the most intelligent animals do not have an ability to communicate with God, nor do they make choices based on God's moral code. *All flesh is not the same flesh* (1 Corinthians 15:39). Animals are programmed by God to do what they do by instinct. On the other hand, mankind was made with a mind that can communicate and reason with God and grasp His spiritual views. Mankind has emotions in order to feel all the pleasures God intended for them. They also have a will with which they can choose to love God and each other, to obey God, and to treat each other with respect. Scripture reveals that mankind was made to have a relationship with their Creator and with each other as indicated in Paul's prayer in Ephesians 3:16-19:

> *That he would grant you, according to the riches of his glory, to be strengthened with might by his Spirit in the inner man; That Christ may dwell in your hearts by faith; that ye, being rooted and grounded in love, may be able to comprehend with all saints what is the breadth, and length, and depth, and height. And to know the love of Christ, which passeth knowledge, that ye might be filled with all the fulness of God.*

God intended to enjoy mankind's fellowship and permit them to enjoy His. They were chosen above all God's creation to model the character of God with their ability to glorify God by thinking purely, loving purely, and choosing purely – a physical, visible representation of the invisible God. This is man's highest purpose on earth. This is what Jesus modelled for us when He came to earth for those short thirty-three years.

God's original purpose for man to occupy, dominate, and enjoy God's Paradise also included marriage between a man and a woman. Genesis 2:18 indicates that man needed someone with whom he could communicate, love, make choices, and worship God: *And the LORD God said, It is not good that the man should be alone; I will make him an help meet for him.*

The animals were not adequate to fill this role as helper, so God created from Adam a special help meet, one made from his own body in the image of God. *And the LORD God caused a deep sleep to fall upon Adam, and he slept: and he took one of his ribs, and closed up the flesh instead thereof; And the rib, which the LORD God had taken from man, made he a woman, and brought her unto the man* (Genesis 2:21-22). Eve was made physically different from Adam in order to multiply the human race. She was to be Adam's wife and the mother of all mankind, equally sharing the image of God, but in a different role. God commanded that man should *leave his father and his mother, and cleave unto his wife: and they shall be one flesh* (Genesis 2:24). He also commanded them to *be fruitful, and multiply, and replenish the earth, and subdue it* (Genesis 1:28).

God's desire for marriage has been corrupted. Everything from divorce and remarriage and homosexuality to bitterness and resentment and lack of communication and love have all been enemies of God's intention for marriage.

Because marriage has been corrupted by sin, God gave us many instructions in the New Testament on how to have the wonderful, agreeable union He planned for man and woman.

> *But I would have you know, that the head of every man is Christ; and the head of the woman is the man; and the head of Christ is God.* (1 Corinthians 11:3)

> *Submitting yourselves one to another in the fear of God.*

> *Wives, submit yourselves unto your own husbands, as unto the Lord. For the husband is the head of the wife, even as Christ is the head of the church: and he is the saviour of the body. Therefore as the church is subject unto Christ, so let the wives be to their own husbands in every thing.*

> *Husbands, love your wives, even as Christ also loved the church, and gave himself for it; that he might sanctify* [set apart] *and cleanse it with the washing of water by the word, that he might present it to himself a glorious church, not having spot, or wrinkle, or any such thing; but that it should be holy and*

*without blemish. So ought men to love their wives
as their own bodies. He that loveth his wife loveth
himself.* (Ephesians 5:21-28)

Just as Christ wants His bride, the Church, to be without blemish, a husband is to spend time with his wife, teaching her from Scripture and praying with her. By doing this, he can help her become a better wife. The husband is the priest of his home. He has a God-given responsibility to study and teach his family the Word of God. We see in 1 Peter 3:1-7 God's instructions to spouses of disobedient or unbelieving husbands and wives:

Likewise, ye wives, be in subjection to your own husbands; that, if any obey not the word, they also may without the word be won by the conversation of the wives; While they behold your chaste conversation coupled with fear. Whose adorning let it not be that outward adorning of plaiting the hair, and of wearing of gold, or of putting on of apparel; But let it be the hidden man of the heart, in that which is not corruptible, even the ornament of a meek and quiet spirit, which is in the sight of God of great price.

For after this manner in the old time the holy women also, who trusted in God, adorned themselves, being in subjection unto their own husbands: Even as Sara obeyed Abraham, calling him lord: whose daughters ye are, as long as ye do well, and are not afraid with any amazement.

Likewise, ye husbands, dwell with them according to knowledge, giving honour unto the wife, as unto the weaker vessel, and as being heirs together of the grace of life; that your prayers be not hindered.

God meant marriage to be a picture of His own relationship to the Church. Christ is the faithful loving husband who protects His wife, the weaker vessel, from the wiles of Satan and leads her into godliness in order to present her spotless before His Father. He gives His life for the Church. The Church is the wife who helps her husband with his goals and plans, building him up with praise and giving him his rightful place as head of the home. She uses all her God-given gifts and talents to meet the needs of her husband and home.

Obviously, God's plan for marriage cannot work unless the husband and the wife are rightly related to their Creator – born again in the Holy Spirit. A marriage between a believer of the gospel and an unbeliever can cause chaos, because they are enemies in the Lord. Marriage is the merging of two bodies into one, just as God joins all believers of the gospel into one body with Christ. A body can never have two heads, because it wouldn't know which to follow. So God chose man to be the head, because Eve was deceived and Adam was not, just as Christ is head of the man and the Church (1 Corinthians 11:3). A man cannot lead his wife into godliness unless he has first been cleansed by the blood of Christ.

Christ has applied the word *submission* to many of our relationships, but it seems we have taken it to an extreme. Submission is about respecting each other in humility and love, and it begins with our submission to God, who owns, loves, and cares for us. Ephesians 5:21 instructs all believers to submit to each other in the fear of God, which leads us to wisdom. *The fear of the LORD is the beginning of wisdom: and the knowledge of the holy is understanding* (Proverbs 9:10). We should be afraid to disappoint our Savior when rising above each other in pride, and we should be afraid of God's earthly chastisements for not submitting to each other. As a military term, *submission* means to get in line behind the leader to accomplish together what needs to be done. Followers should do all they can to support their leader with the goal of success. Leaders are expected to get their instructions from God and lovingly guide followers in completing them.

Men and women are different. They need to accept these differences, because God displays a different side of Himself through each of them. In general, men display the leader/protector side of God. They tend to think first and feel later. Women are likely to display the compassionate side of God. They tend to feel first and think later. Men and women were not made to be the same, although God says in Galatians that they are equal in His sight. *There is neither Jew nor Greek, there is neither bond nor free, there is neither male nor female: for ye are all one in Christ Jesus* (Galatians 3:28). In our relationship with Christ, we are spiritually equal. We are equally responsible to put our faith in the blood of Christ and study His Word. We equally receive blessing for our obedience and chastisement for our disobedience. God uses us equally in His kingdom, but in different roles. Someone once said that men and women are like chocolate and nuts. They are good alone, but even better when together.

God's original plan for mankind was altered by the choices Adam and Eve made. Eve was deceived when she stepped out from under Adam's God-given headship. She was not made to take ultimate responsibility. *For Adam was first formed, then Eve. And Adam was not deceived, but the woman being deceived was in the transgression* (1 Timothy 2:13-14). On the other hand, Adam stepped out of his leadership role of protecting his wife by following Eve into disobedience. He actually led her to sin by not leading her away from it.

Christ, the second Adam, is our only hope for restoring God's order. *For since by man came death, by man came also the resurrection of the dead. For as in Adam all die, even so in Christ shall all be made alive* (1 Corinthians 15:21-22). It is impossible for men or women to do what God intended them to do without the Holy Spirit dwelling in them. A preacher once said, "Until a man is mastered by Christ, he is not a true man – not the man God created Him to be." The same can be said about women.

Children

> Lo, children are an heritage of the LORD: and the fruit of the womb is his reward. As arrows are in the hand of a mighty man; so are children of the youth. Happy is the man that hath his quiver full of them: they shall not be ashamed. (Psalm 127:3-5)

As in the parable of the talents in Matthew 25:14-30, parents are made stewards or guardians of the children God has gifted to them and will be judged on how much they invest in their children's lives. If raised in a godly fashion, children will bring much joy and blessing to their parents (Proverbs 20:7; 31:28).

We are admonished to be like children when it comes to faith in Christ, because children are very trusting and want to please their parents. They can be led to Christ at an early age because of their trusting confidence in adults. They can just as easily be led into evil for the same reason. Fathers: as priest of your home, take advantage of the time you have with your young children to give them a godly appetite. My father faithfully read and explained the Bible to us and prayed for us every day he was able, and on the days he couldn't, my mother would read to us. To this day, all ten of their children are serving the Lord, and they have trained their children in the same manner. By God's grace it is possible to raise God-loving children.

In spite of their perceived innocence, children are born in sin with Adam's nature. Even before they can speak, they show their defiance, and "no" seems to be their first word. While we must have much patience and grace for our children, we ought to start teaching them from the time they're born. As Paul said to Timothy: *But continue thou in the things which thou hast learned and hast been assured of . . . that from a child thou hast known the holy scriptures, which are able to make thee wise unto salvation through faith which is in Christ Jesus* (2 Timothy 3:14-15).

Children are commanded to obey their parents, and this is the first commandment that has a blessing attached to it. This makes sense, because obedience extends your life by keeping you from danger and sin, which could shorten your life. Once we are out of the home, God expects us to never stop honoring our parents with love and respect.

Children are great imitators. They copy everything their parents do. I once had a student in my classroom who wanted badly to be like his dad. His dad was very funny, in a proper way, but the young son didn't have the maturity to know when to be funny, and he constantly disrupted the classroom. It was very frustrating to him that while his dad could make so many people laugh, he only got in trouble for his jokes.

Another student was always angry. At first, I wondered how a six-year-old could be so angry, until I spent time in his home. In a parent/teacher meeting, I brought up the anger issue, because the boy was making more enemies in school than friends. I suggested to the parents that their son was learning this anger from someone else. The father immediately became angry with me for saying he had an angry son. Years later, that man drove his family away because of his anger and bitterness.

So you see, you can determine whether you want loving children who openly share their thoughts with you, or harsh, angry children who distance themselves from you. Act out what you want your children to be, and they will copy you. That's why God has said: *And, ye fathers provoke not your children to wrath: but bring them up in the nurture* [training/correction] *and admonition* [warning] *of the Lord* (Ephesians 6:4). Making unreasonable and inconsistent demands on your children will only frustrate them, which results in bitterness and anger. I wonder if some parents put more care and effort into raising their crops than they do in raising their children. Do we want to raise a crop of undesirable children?

Husbands and wives, I admonish you to prayerfully decide what kind of children you want to raise, and then go to the Bible to find out how to do it. Over and over, you will find that love and kindness is the answer. Usually, how a husband treats his wife is how his sons will treat women, and how the wife treats her husband is how the daughter will treat men – unless, of course, the children prayerfully seek the Lord to change them. I have seen that most children view God as they view their father.

God's purpose for mankind is still to bear His image – through our own lives, through our relationships with our spouses, and through our relationships with our children. Because of sin, we do need restraints – God-given restraints. Parents restrain children from acting out their sinful nature in the home, and teachers restrain children from acting out their sinful nature in the school. We were all born with a conscience as our inner restraint, which needs to be developed as we grow older. We have God-ordained civil law or government to control our sinfulness in the social world, and we have the local church as our spiritual restraint. But, the first and foremost restraint is the Holy Spirit, who works through our conscience. Are you listening to Him?

Prayer

Father in heaven, help us be the mirrors You intend us to be, showing forth Your glory and grace to all those around us. May we always be open for Your empowering Spirit to fill us and work through us, for our corrupted flesh could never reflect Your goodness. Change our thoughts to bring about Your will. Change our actions to show people who You are, and use our mouths to preach Your gospel. Give us the grace to love our spouses and children as You do and to train them to love You. May our lives bring glory to the name of Jesus Christ in our homes, our schools, our churches, and in public. In the name of Jesus we ask this. Amen.

Chapter 8

SIN AND SALVATION

Soteriology

For since by man came death, by man came also the resurrection of the dead. (1 Corinthians 15:21)

Introduction

If you look forward to eternity in heaven, then it is critical to know and understand who Jesus Christ is and what He has done. In the Gospel of John, we find the longest recorded prayer of our Lord Jesus Christ in the Holy Scriptures. A portion of this prayer is, *Sanctify them through thy truth: thy word is truth* (John 17:17). In the Greek, that word *sanctify* means to set them apart for God and His purposes. In this chapter, we will look at what sin is and how we are saved from the consequences of sin, based on truth found in the Gospel of John. Let's take a look at what the Amish teach.

What the Amish Teach

Excerpts from the Dordrecht Confession of Faith

Article 2

"We believe and confess, according to the holy Scriptures, that these our first parents, Adam and Eve, did not continue long in this glorious state in which they were created, but that they, seduced by the subtlety and deceit of the serpent, and the envy of the devil, transgressed the high commandment of God and became disobedient to their Creator; through which disobedience sin has come into the world, and death by sin, which has thus passed upon all men, for that all have sinned, and, hence, brought upon themselves the wrath of God, and condemnation; for which reason they were of God driven out of Paradise, or the pleasure garden, to till the earth, in sorrow to eat of it, and to eat their bread in the sweat of their face, till they should return to the earth, from which they were taken; and that they, therefore, through this one sin, became so ruined, separated, and estranged from God, that they, neither through themselves, nor through any of their descendants, nor through angels, nor men, nor any other creature in heaven or on earth, could be raised up, redeemed, or reconciled to God, but would have had to be eternally lost, had not God, in compassion for His creatures, made provision for it, and interposed with His love and mercy.

Article 3

The belief that with God "there was yet a means of reconciliation [being made right], namely, the immaculate [spotless] Lamb, the Son of God, who had been foreordained thereto before the foundation of the world, and . . . that He by His coming, would redeem, liberate, and raise the fallen race of man from their sin, guilt, and unrighteousness."

Article 4

Jesus was "yielded up as a sacrifice and offering, for a sweet savor unto God, yea, for the consolation, redemption, and salvation of all mankind. . . . He is the Son of the living God, in whom alone consist all our hope, consolation, redemption, and salvation, which we neither may nor must seek in any other. . . . [Jesus] was crucified, dead, was buried, and on the third day, rose from the dead, and ascended to heaven; and that He sits on the right hand of God the Majesty on high, whence He will come again to judge the quick and the dead."

Article 6

"For neither baptism, supper, church [membership], nor any other outward ceremony, can without faith, regeneration, change or renewing of life, avail anything to please God or to obtain of Him any consolation or promise of salvation; but we must go to God with an upright heart, and in perfect faith, and believe in Jesus Christ, as the Scripture says, and testifies of Him; through which faith we obtain forgiveness of sins, are sanctified, justified, and made children of God, yea, partake of His mind, nature, and image, as being born again of God from above, through incorruptible seed."

Martyrs Mirror, First Confession

"For although the blessed Lord Jesus Christ is the only meritorious [worthy] cause of the justification of man, their adoption by God as His children, and the foundation of their eternal salvation, God the heavenly Father . . . has nevertheless been pleased to impute the merits of His Son Jesus Christ to man, and make him partaker of the same, through the means of faith in His only, and only-begotten Son . . . according to the testimony of John, who says: *He* [that is, Christ] *came unto his own, and his own received him not. But as many as received him, to them gave he power to become the sons of God, even to them that believe on his name: which were born, not of blood, nor of the will of the flesh, nor of the will of man, but of God* (John 1:11-13)."

The statements regarding salvation found in the *Dordrecht Confession of Faith* and *Martyrs Mirror* are accurate, but not particularly clear. Sometimes there is a disconnect between what we say we believe and what we practice. And sometimes, unfortunately, we don't read these important books, or even the Bible, with a real passion to understand, instead taking the easy way out and trusting that others are taking care of these matters for us.

The *Dordrecht Confession of Faith* and *Martyrs Mirror* use the phrases "Son of the living God, in whom *alone*" and "Jesus Christ is the *only* meritorious cause," which tell us we can do nothing to earn our way to heaven. It is only through Jesus Christ, His sacrifice, and His shed blood that we are adopted as children of God. This then begs the questions: Do we really believe what we say we believe? Do we truly know, in a personal way, what Jesus Christ has accomplished on our behalf?

The Bible is the truth and has not been distorted by the corruption of the fall of man, as recorded in Genesis chapter 3. As you study, be sure to open the Word of God in a language that you understand and pray that God would open your heart to the truth of His Word.

What the Scriptures Teach

What Is Sin?

It became obvious in the Old Testament that man could neither keep the law of God nor do anything to earn salvation. In fact, the law was really given to man to show that we could never obey on our own. *Wherefore the law was our schoolmaster to bring us unto Christ, that we might be justified by faith* (Galatians 3:24).

Consider what the apostle Paul wrote in the New Testament to the church at Rome:

> *Now we know that what things soever the law saith, it saith to them who are under the law: that every mouth may be stopped, and all the world may become guilty before God.*
>
> *Therefore by the deeds of the law there shall be no flesh be justified in his sight: for by the law is the knowledge of sin. But now the righteousness of God without the law is manifested, being witnessed by the law and the prophets; Even the righteousness of God which is by faith of Jesus Christ unto all and upon all them that believe: for there is no difference:*
>
> *For all have sinned, and come short of the glory of God;*

Being justified freely by his grace through the
redemption that is in Christ Jesus. (Romans 3:19-24)

Later, Paul tells the Romans that *whatsoever is not of faith is sin* (Romans 14:23). And even James says, *to him that knoweth to do good, and doeth it not, to him it is sin* (James 4:17).

The Entrance of Sin into the World

God's plan for man and woman to live in perfection forever with Him came to an abrupt end in the garden. The Almighty gave them just one restriction to exercise their will, and they chose wrongly. The Bible makes it clear that Eve was deceived into disobedience, but Adam, for reasons not made known, *chose* to disobey. *Adam was not deceived, but the woman being deceived was in the transgression* (1 Timothy 2:14).

Satan doesn't usually come face-to-face when tempting us to do wrong. He is the great deceiver, at times even hiding behind those we trust. *For Satan himself is transformed into an angel of light* (2 Corinthians 11:14). That is how he came to Eve. He hid within the snake and talked her into believing the same lie that brought him down. Revelation 12:9 calls him *that old serpent . . . the Devil, and Satan.* Satan said they could *be as gods,* deciding for themselves what was right or wrong (Genesis 3:5). He continues, even to this day, to carry out his goal of destroying as much of God's creation as possible, for *he was a murderer from the beginning* and *the father of* [lies] (John 8:44). He walks about *as a roaring lion . . . seeking whom he may devour* (1 Peter 5:8). Human beings were not made to operate under their own power. They can only function properly according to their Creator's direction – in accordance with His Word.

The Result of Man's Sin

God said Adam and Eve would *surely die* for their disobedience

(Genesis 2:17). To die is to be separated from God; *but your iniquities have separated between you and your God* (Isaiah 59:2). First, their fellowship with God was severed. They were now under *the wrath of God* (Ephesians 5:6). *For the wrath of God is revealed from heaven against all ungodliness and unrighteousness of men* (Romans 1:18). They would eventually be separated from their bodies to *die, and return to their dust* (Psalm 104:29). The *devil that deceived them* would be *cast into the lake of fire . . . and whosoever was not found written in the book of life was cast into the lake of fire,* where they would be eternally separated from God (Revelation 20:10, 15).

Adam and Eve were *dead in trespasses and sins* (Ephesians 2:1), just like a branch separated from a tree. A tree branch doesn't show its death immediately. It looks green and healthy for quite a while before it shrivels and decays back into the ground. Adam and Eve didn't look dead immediately, but they were. They were separated from their Source of Life, left to their own resources, blinded in unbelief by the *god of this world* [Satan] (2 Corinthians 4:4). *He that committeth sin is of the devil,* and because of him, *the whole world lieth in wickedness* (1 John 3:8; 5:19). In a very short time, Adam and Eve, who were children of the Most High and holy Creator of life, chose to become the children of the lowest and most evil destroyer of life.

Was God justified in allowing this? Of course! He was their Creator, their owner, their highest authority. His holiness demanded righteousness. All sin results in death, as the Lord said: *When a righteous man turneth away from his righteousness, and committeth iniquity, and dieth in them; for his iniquity that he hath done shall he die* (Ezekiel 18:26). The Almighty's pure eyes *canst not look on iniquity* (Habakkuk 1:13). This helps us understand why James wrote, *For whosoever shall keep the whole law, and yet offend in one point, he is guilty of all* (James 2:10). God's only recourse was to cast Adam and Eve out of

His presence, for His law says that *the wages of sin is death* (Romans 6:23).

Sadly, Adam's *death passed upon all men, for that all have sinned* (Romans 5:12). Adam lost the holiness of God for the whole human race, for all come from his blood (Acts 17:26). God's original plan for them to prosper in perfection died. Romans 1:18-2:1 describes our human nature in strikingly clear detail and declares us all *without excuse.*

Genesis 3:7 tells us *the eyes of them both were opened, and they knew that they were naked; and they sewed fig leaves together, and made themselves aprons.* What a lame, human attempt to make themselves acceptable to God. Like Adam, we tend to hide our wrongdoings with outward measures. Whether it be by our behavior, our words, or the way we dress, we cannot hide our sinful nature from God and expect to be accepted by Him. No matter what we do to cover up, our soul stands naked before the Lord.

It was the inner man – the part made in God's likeness – that needed to be cleansed. God gave Adam and Eve their chance to confess their sin and receive forgiveness when He *called unto Adam, and said unto him, Where art thou?* (Genesis 3:9). Sadly, they clung to their pride and cast their blame on one another, on the serpent, and on God. As a result, the whole world was cursed, and they remained in their sin, absolutely helpless against the powers of evil:

> And the LORD God said unto the serpent, Because thou hast done this, thou art cursed above all cattle, and above every beast of the field; upon thy belly shalt thou go, and dust shalt thou eat all the days of thy life:

> And I will put enmity between thee and the woman, and between thy seed and her seed: it shall bruise thy head, and thou shalt bruise his heel.

*Unto the woman he said, I will greatly multiply thy sorrow
and thy conception; in sorrow thou shalt bring forth children; and thy desire shall be to thy husband, and he shall
rule over thee.*

*And unto Adam he said, Because thou hast hearkened
unto the voice of thy wife, and hast eaten of the tree, of
which I commanded thee, saying, Thou shalt not eat of
it: cursed is the ground for thy sake; in sorrow shalt thou
eat of it all the days of thy life; thorns also and thistles
shall it bring forth to thee; and thou shalt eat the herb
of the field; in the sweat of thy face shalt thou eat bread,
till thou return unto the ground; for out of it wast thou
taken: for dust thou art, and unto dust shalt thou return.*
(Genesis 3:14-19)

They were driven out of their home and away from the presence of their Creator, without any means of return. *Therefore
the LORD God sent him forth from the garden of Eden, to till
the ground from whence he was taken. So he drove out the man;
and he placed at the east of the garden of Eden Cherubims, and
a flaming sword which turned every way, to keep the way of the
tree of life* (Genesis 3:23-24).

The Atonement

God is first of all holy, but He is also a very gracious and loving
God. In spite of the fairness of His judgment, He mercifully
provided a way of escape from the condemnation of their sin,
for God is *not willing that any should perish, but that all should
come to repentance* (2 Peter 3:9). At that moment, God killed an
animal in order to cover Adam and Eve's nakedness, so they
could properly stand in His presence. Innocent blood was shed
in order to cover them.

Even from the foundation of the world, God planned to

provide a substitute, an acceptable Savior, who would give His life in exchange for all mankind, freeing them from the power of Satan, sin, and death. This redemption (buying back) was accomplished *with the precious blood of Christ, as of a lamb without blemish and without spot: who verily was foreordained before the foundation of the world* (1 Peter 1:19-20). The innocent substitute would willingly shed His blood in order to clothe us in His righteousness (Romans 4:3-5), so we could be brought back into the family of God. He *gave himself for our sins, that he might deliver us from this present evil world, according to the will of God and our Father* (Galatians 1:4).

In Leviticus 17:11, God said that *the life of the flesh is in the blood: and I have given it to you upon the altar to make an atonement for your souls: for it is the blood that maketh an atonement for the soul.* God instructed them to continue killing animals on an altar as a covering over their sin until the day when the *woman's seed*, the Savior, would come to deliver them by offering His own life's blood in exchange for theirs, for *without* [the] *shedding of blood* [there] *is no remission* [of sin] (Hebrews 9:22).

The blood of animals was only a picture of what was to come – *a figure for the time then present . . . that could not make* [them] *that did the service perfect, as pertaining to the conscience* (Hebrews 9:9). They still carried guilt. It was a temporary cleansing they had to repeat year after year to delay God's judgment until the true and final Day of Atonement; but God did take into account their faith in the future Lamb of God, who would spill His blood in exchange for theirs (Romans 4:3; John 1:29). God will not tolerate man's effort to make himself acceptable to Him. Man can only come to God by God's way, for Jesus said, *I am the way, the truth, and the life: no man cometh unto the Father, but by me* (John 14:6).

Adam's offspring, Cain and Abel, had to decide for themselves whether or not to believe God's promise of redemption. As we see in Genesis chapter 4, Abel came to God with a lamb, the firstling of his flock, and shed its blood on the altar. Abel demonstrated his faith by *offering a more excellent sacrifice than Cain* (Hebrews 11:4). On the other hand, Cain *brought of the fruit of the ground,* but the Lord *had not respect* for Cain's offering (Genesis 4:3, 5). He obviously came to God with his own idea of an offering and was rejected. Cain's pride led to an unrepentant attitude, jealousy, and the murder of his brother (Genesis 4:8).

All through the Old Testament, God graciously gave mankind shadows, or pictures, to remind them to put their faith in the coming Savior (Hebrews 10:1) – shadows like God's provision of escape for Noah and his family (Genesis 6-9), Abraham sacrificing his son (Genesis 22:1-19), the serpent on the brass pole (Numbers 21:6-9), manna (Exodus 16:11-36), the law, the tabernacle (Exodus 25-27), and the Passover lamb (Exodus 12:1-13:10), to name a few. These shadows could never have saved them from their sin. They only pointed forward to the day when the true Messiah would come. The Messiah, Jesus Christ, would become the *second Adam* (1 Corinthians 15:20-24, 45-48; Romans 5:14-15). He would be the true image of God, replacing the first Adam and showing us what we were created to be.

The first Adam gave us a living soul. The second Adam gives us a living spirit (1 Corinthians 15:22, 45). Christ is the only one qualified to give back to mankind that which the first Adam lost. By allowing His own innocent Son to die as the ultimate sacrifice for sin, God is able to clothe us in His righteousness (Romans 3:22-26).

What Is Salvation
We read in John 15:16 that God takes the first step concerning

our salvation – *Ye have not chosen me, but I have chosen you.* And we have already seen that all of us are inexcusable sinners before God – lost and wandering (Romans 1:18-3:20). Luke 19:10 tells us that *the Son of man is come to seek and to save that which was lost.* God takes the first step, because He knows we will not (Romans 3:11). God's purpose for every man, woman, and child is that we *should be holy and without blame before him in love.* He prearranged for our adoption by Jesus Christ *before the foundation of the world* (Ephesians 1:4-5; Romans 8:28-30), yet He makes us responsible to respond to Him with repentance and faith. The jailer in Acts 16:30-31 cried, *What must I do to be saved?* The answer from the apostles was, *Believe on the Lord Jesus Christ, and thou shalt be saved, and thy house.*

Salvation is the change from our natural life to a spiritual life which God meant for us to have on this earth and for eternity, not something we *might* have in the hereafter (Romans 8:12-16). The Jesus of the Holy Scriptures calls us to know Him deeply, love Him with all our hearts, walk closely with Him, and make Him the central focus of our lives. One of the religious leaders of the day asked Jesus a question: *Master, which is the great commandment in the law? Jesus said unto him, Thou shalt love the Lord thy God with all thy heart, and with all thy soul, and with all thy mind. This is the first and great commandment* (Matthew 22:36-38). This is the difference between knowing about Jesus and entering into a personal relationship with our living Savior. Knowing *about* Jesus is only knowing the facts that we learn, but this does not always impact our lives. Knowing Jesus *by faith* moves Him from our head to our hearts and dramatically changes our lives. *Therefore if any man be in Christ, he is a new creature: old things are passed away; behold, all things become new* (2 Corinthians 5:17).

John 1:29 states that Jesus Christ is the perfect *Lamb of God, which taketh away the sins of the world,* because He met the demands of the Law for the atoning sacrifice – a male without blemish, offered voluntarily, and killed by the pouring out of his blood (Leviticus 1:3-5; Hebrews 12:24). He is the only person without sin and worthy to die in our place. Why was a better sacrifice necessary? Because *it is not possible that the blood of bulls and goats should take away sins* (Hebrews 10:4). That was the condition of the old covenant, which did not satisfy God's law. A perfect sacrifice and a new covenant were found in the person of Jesus Christ – the only one who could satisfy God's wrath and justice. *For what the law could not do, in that it was weak through the flesh, God sending his own Son in the likeness of sinful flesh, and for sin, condemned sin in the flesh: that the righteousness of the law might be fulfilled in us, who walk not after the flesh, but after the Spirit* (Romans 8:3-4).

On the evening before Jesus was crucified, while eating with his disciples, He lifted a cup, saying: *This cup is the new testament* [covenant] *in my blood: this do ye, as oft as ye drink it, in remembrance of me* (1 Corinthians 11:25). The shed blood of Jesus on the cross cleanses us of our sins once for all, and *if thou shalt confess with thy mouth the Lord Jesus, and shalt believe in thine heart that God hath raised him from the dead, thou shalt be saved* (Romans 10:9). Just as the Israelites were delivered from the hand of the death angel by the blood of a lamb in Exodus 12:21-51, so are we delivered from the hand of Satan, sin, and death through the blood of the Lamb of God (Hebrews 9:14). Speaking of Jesus, the apostle Peter said: *Neither is there salvation in any other: for there is none other name under heaven given among men, whereby we must be saved* (Acts 4:12). Jesus is our perfect Savior!

Why do we need a savior? Dead means dead. When we are dead, we are unable to bring ourselves to life spiritually. Our destiny is hell. Only the atoning sacrifice of Jesus Christ is able to accomplish the miracle of giving everlasting life. We *who were dead in trespasses and sins* were made alive by Jesus Christ (Ephesians 2:1). *Not by works of righteousness which we have done, but according to his mercy he saved us, by the washing of regeneration, and renewing of the Holy Ghost; Which he shed on us abundantly through Jesus Christ our Saviour* (Titus 3:5-6).

Right from the beginning of the church, we see the apostles preaching that we should *repent and be baptized every one of you in the name of Jesus Christ for the remission* [forgiveness] *of sins, and ye shall receive the gift of the Holy Ghost* (Acts 2:38). *Repent* simply means to turn and go in the opposite direction. When we come to the realization that we cannot possibly make ourselves acceptable to God, we turn *from* what we've always believed in order to turn *to* what God says is true about Jesus Christ. We say to God, "You're right, and I'm wrong. I'm going to obey your instructions from now on," and then trust Christ as your righteousness and not yourself. One of your first acts of obedience should be baptism, which identifies you with Christ's death, burial, and resurrection. Then, join a body of believers where the Word of God is soundly taught. Jesus should be at the center of your life. Knowing Him should fuel a hunger within you to love God, love His Word, love His people, and love sharing the gospel with the lost. Seek Him in the Scriptures with all your heart. He alone is our only hope of salvation. Are you a child of God?

> I would not work my soul to save,
> For this my Lord hath done;
> But I would work like any slave
> For love of His dear Son.[4]

He that hath the Son hath life; and he that hath not the Son of God hath not life. These things have I

---

4 Author unknown.

written unto you that believe on the name of the Son
*of God; that ye may **know** that ye have eternal life,*
and that ye may believe on the name of the Son of
God. (1 John 5:12-13)

Prayer

Thank You, Father, for giving us truth in Your Word. We do not even understand how sinful we are, and Your Word teaches us that we can't do anything of ourselves to be cleansed. We are lost, but You, Father, have provided a way for us through the blood of Your Son. Thank You for loving us enough to send Him to suffer and die on our behalf. Our hearts bow down before You in love and admiration for Your goodness and Your righteousness. Thank you for saving us through Your Son, Jesus Christ. Amen.

Chapter 9

THE END TIMES

Eschatology

Watch therefore: for ye know not what hour your Lord doth come. But know this, that if the goodman of the house had known in what watch the thief would come, he would have watched, and would not have suffered his house to be broken up. Therefore be ye also ready: for in such an hour as ye think not the Son of man cometh. (Matthew 24:42-44)

Introduction

We now come to the concluding message of the Bible – the Revelation of Jesus Christ. The book of Revelation is the fulfilment of God's plan for mankind which began in Genesis. Every book in the Bible is important for our spiritual growth, though Genesis is the foundation for understanding the whole Bible, and Revelation shows us where we're headed. It is the crowning moment of joy for God the Father, when His Son receives and presents His bride, the Church, to Him. It is the glorious conclusion of salvation to all those who have responded to the call of God by repentance and faith in the death, burial, and resurrection of the Son.

There are many mysteries God has chosen not to tell us, yet

here in Revelation, He graciously lets us know what is to come at the end of time, so we can be prepared for the future. Take a look at Psalm 103 and read the comforting promises made to those who fear God. To fear Him is to believe His every word and dedicate your life to serving Him. Fearing God in this life will give us confidence in the next.

While teaching in an Amish school, I was warned by the bishop never to mention the book of Revelation in morning devotions. Sadly, it is a book that is widely ignored by most religions because of its seemingly strange and fearful happenings which they cannot understand. It *should* be fearful to those who do not have faith in Jesus Christ, and it should turn them from trusting anything else for their salvation. God has revealed to us many clear signs to warn us of the coming end, which we will discuss in this chapter. He has told us what to look for so that Christians will not lose heart but will remain diligent in serving Christ until He comes. Matthew 24 says to *watch . . .* and be *ready: for in such an hour as ye think not the Son of man cometh.*

What the Amish Teach

Since groups of Amish believers differ from one another, what is held as true for one group can be different for another group. However, it is interesting to note that when it comes to the end of the world, almost all Amish share the same view.

The clearest Amish viewpoint on the end times comes from the *Dordrecht Confession of Faith*, which was created and upheld on April 21, 1632, at a Dutch Mennonite conference. While not all Amish have read this document, many bishops have or can trace their doctrinal positions back to this historical document. It is composed of eighteen articles, the last of which speaks of the end of the world, under the heading, "Of the Resurrection of the Dead, and the Last Judgment." It states:

"Finally, concerning the resurrection of the dead, we confess with the mouth, and believe with the heart, according to Scripture, that in the last day all men who shall have died, and fallen asleep, shall be awaked and quickened [brought to life], and shall rise again, through the incomprehensible power of God; and that they, together with those who then will still be alive, and who shall be changed in the twinkling of an eye, at the sound of the last trump, shall be placed before the judgment seat of Christ, and the good be separated from the wicked; that then everyone shall receive in his own body according to that he hath done, whether it be good or evil; and that the good or pious, as the blessed, shall be taken up with Christ, and shall enter into life eternal, and obtain that joy, which eye hath not seen, nor ear heard, neither hath entered into the heart of man, to reign and triumph with Christ forever and ever. Matthew 22:30-31; Daniel 12:12; Job 19:26-27; Matthew 25:31; John 5:28; 2 Corinthians 5:10; 1 Corinthians 15; Revelation 20:12; 1 Thessalonians 4:15; 1 Corinthians 2:9.

"And that, on the other hand, the wicked or impious, as accursed, shall be cast into outer darkness, yea, into the everlasting pains of hell, where their worm shall not die, nor their fire be quenched, and where they, according to holy Scripture, can nevermore expect any hope, comfort, or redemption. Mark 9:44; Revelation 14:11."

This view is common in many Amish churches today, and while much of it is scriptural, it leaves out some issues and topics raised elsewhere in the Scriptures. It is a general view of the end times, and it behooves us to know more about what will happen in the end.

While the *Dordrecht Confession of Faith* does not say it specifically, history attests that the Amish view is a preterist view of the book of Revelation. That means they believe Revelation speaks mostly about events that have happened after the life, death, and resurrection of Jesus Christ in the first century, and does not address much of what will happen after Christ returns for the Church. When it comes to the *millennium* (the thousand-year reign of Christ on earth), the historic position of the Amish has always been *amillennialism*, which is natural for those who believe in preterism. Millennialism is the belief that Christ will reign on earth with the saints for a thousand years prior to the final judgment. Amillennialism, on the other hand, is the rejection of that belief.

What the Scriptures Teach

We will take a broad approach that looks at what we should watch for, know about, and be ready for, relating to the return of Christ, and offer Scripture verses for further study on your own.

Be Watchful and Ready

In chapter 24 of Matthew, Jesus is talking to His disciples as they overlook Jerusalem. They pointed to the temple buildings, and He told them there would come a time when not one stone would be left upon another.

Following this, His disciples came to Him privately to ask when these things would take place and *what shall be the sign of thy coming, and of the end of the world?* (Matthew 24:3). Before He got into the details, He told them to *take heed that no man deceive you,* because many would be deceived (Matthew 24:4). The disciples wanted to know what to watch for, and Jesus warned them not to be deceived. This is also a warning for us to be watchful and to carefully search the Scriptures so as not to be deceived.

We Live in the End Times

Often people tend to limit their concept of "end times" to the end of the world, but humanity has actually lived in the end times for almost 2,000 years. Hebrews 1:2 confirms this: [God] *Hath **in these last days** spoken unto us by his Son, whom he hath appointed heir of all things, by whom also he made the worlds.* While we don't know the exact time the book of Hebrews was written, we do know it was sometime after Christ's ascension and sometime before the destruction of Jerusalem (AD 70), because the temple was still standing. Here are some more signs the apostles were told to watch for in Matthew 24:

> *For many shall come in my name, saying, I am Christ; and shall deceive many.*
>
> *Ye shall hear of wars and rumours of wars: see that ye be not troubled: for all these things must come to pass, but the end is not yet.*
>
> *For nation shall rise against nation, and kingdom against kingdom: and there shall be famines, and pestilences, and earthquakes, in diverse places.* (Matthew 24:5-7)

Luke 21:11 also mentions earthquakes and says that *fearful sights and great signs shall there be from heaven.*

While we could easily compile a book on this verse alone, let's just use earthquakes to put things into perspective. The United States Geological Survey (USGS)[5] estimates "several million earthquakes occur in the world each year. Many go

---

5   USGS is the federal agency responsible for recording and reporting earthquake activity in the United States. *www.earthquake.usgs.gov/earthquakes/eqarchives.*

undetected because they hit remote areas or have very small magnitudes. The National Earthquake Information Center (NEIC) now locates about 50 earthquakes each day or about 20,000 a year." In a 2014 interview with *Live Science*, Thorne Lay, a professor at the University of California, Santa Cruz, pointed out an increase in larger quakes saying, "Between 1900 and 2004, the average yearly rate of quakes of magnitude 8 and larger was 0.65. In the past 10 years, that rate jumped to 1.8 – an increase of almost a factor of 3. But only the biggest quakes are becoming more frequent. There isn't a similar rise in smaller earthquakes."

Matthew 24:8 says that *all these are the beginning of sorrows,* and John 16:21 further compares all of these things to birth pangs: *A woman when she is in travail hath sorrow, because her hour is come: but as soon as she is delivered of the child, she remembereth no more the anguish, for joy that a man is born into the world.* Just as a woman in labor knows the baby is on the way, when Christians see these things come about with growing intensity, we know the Lord's coming is nearer. And just like birth pangs end when the baby is born and the mother welcomes her child with joy, we will be filled with joy when He arrives.

Descriptions and signs of the end times are sprinkled throughout Scripture. Luke 21:25 states: *And there shall be signs in the sun, and in the moon, and in the stars; and upon the earth distress of nations, with perplexity; the sea and the waves roaring.* But the signs of the end times aren't limited to natural events and happenings. Signs will also be evident in society.

In the end times people will become evil like in the days of Noah, when *they were eating and drinking, marrying and giving in marriage, until the day that Noe entered into the ark* (Matthew 24:37-38). In 2 Timothy 3:1-5, the apostle Paul says people will *be lovers of their own selves, covetous* [lovers of money] . . . *lovers of pleasures,* and will be *boasters, proud,* and *unholy.* Children will be *disobedient to parents.* In 1 Timothy 4:1, we learn *that in the latter times some shall depart from the faith, giving heed to seducing spirits, and doctrines of devils.* These earthly catastrophes and behaviors of people will be common in the end times.

The Rapture

Not all Christians believe there will be a rapture, but many do. The rapture idea was popularized in the 1830s. The term refers to a snatching up to heaven of true Christians while they are still alive, along with those who have already died. In the rapture, it is said that Jesus will come in the air and catch up the Church from the earth. Those in Christ will be physically raised into the skies, given new bodies free of aging, disease, and sin and taken home to heaven as they are. In Matthew 24:36, Jesus said no one will know the day or the hour – not even the angels. Only God knows. Views on the timing of the rapture differ, but the one thing they have in common is that they are believed to happen around the time of the Great Tribulation.

> **Pre-tribulation rapture:** The pre-tribulation view places the rapture before the seven years of the Great Tribulation. In Revelation 4:1, John sees an open door in heaven and hears a voice like a trumpet, which says, *Come up hither.* After this point, the church is not mentioned.

> **Mid-tribulation rapture:** This view says the rapture occurs midway through the seven years of Great Tribulation, when the two prophets ascend to heaven (Revelation 11:11-12).

> **Post-tribulation rapture:** This view places the rapture at the end of the seven vial judgments (Revelation 16:17-21).

The rapture theory is based on the following Scriptures:

*And to wait for his Son from heaven, whom he raised from the dead, even Jesus, which delivered us from the **wrath** to come.* (1 Thessalonians 1:10)

*For God hath not appointed us to **wrath**, but to obtain salvation by our Lord Jesus Christ.* (1 Thessalonians 5:9)

For the Lord himself shall descend from heaven with a shout, with the voice of the archangel, and with the trump of God: and the dead in Christ shall rise first: Then we which are alive and remain shall be caught up together with them in the clouds, to meet the Lord in the air: and so shall we ever be with the Lord. Wherefore comfort one another with these words. (1 Thessalonians 4:16-18)

The Great Tribulation

For then shall be great tribulation, such as was not since the beginning of the world to this time, no, nor ever shall be. (Matthew 24:21)

The Bible clearly speaks of a great tribulation. This time of trouble and distress will occur just prior to the return of Christ for His 1,000-year reign on earth. Based on the forty-two months mentioned in Revelation 13:5 and *a time and times and the dividing of time* in the prophecy found in Daniel 7:25, the tribulation will last for seven years. For those who want to do the math, plenty of information is available to help you reach the same conclusion. This seven-year period will be a time so severe that *except those days should be shortened, there should no flesh be saved: but for the elect's sake those days shall be shortened* (Matthew 24:22).

The book of Revelation describes this as a time when God's wrath is poured out on the world that has rejected Him. Judgments are depicted in the seven seals (Revelation 6:1-17), seven trumpets (Revelation 8:6-13; 11:15-19), and seven bowls/vials (Revelation 16:1-21). All this culminates in what is known as the battle of Armageddon, when the Lord returns and comes against those who have rejected Him.

The following are other scriptures that relate to the great tribulation:

> *And at that time shall Michael stand up, the great prince which standeth for the children of thy people: and there shall be a time of trouble, such as never was since there was a nation even to that same time.* (Daniel 12:1)

> *For then shall be great tribulation, such as was not since the beginning of the world to this time, no, nor ever shall be. . . . Immediately after the tribulation of those days shall the sun be darkened, and the moon shall not give her light, and the stars shall fall from heaven, and the powers of the heavens shall be shaken.* (Matthew 24:21, 29)

> *But in those days, after that tribulation, the sun shall be darkened, and the moon shall not give her light.* (Mark 13:24)

The Antichrist and Mark of the Beast

> *Little children, it is the last time: and as ye have heard that antichrist shall come, even now are there many antichrists; whereby we know that it is the last time.* (1 John 2:18)

> *And the beast which I saw was like unto a leopard,*

*and his feet were as the feet of a bear, and his mouth
as the mouth of a lion; and the dragon gave him
his power, and his seat, and great authority. And I
saw one of his heads as it were wounded to death;
and his deadly wound was healed; and all the earth
wondered after the beast. And they worshipped the
dragon which gave power unto the beast: and they
worshipped the beast, saying, Who is like unto the
beast? who is able to make war with him? And there
was given unto him a mouth speaking great things
and blasphemies; and power was given unto him
to continue forty and two months. And he opened
his mouth in blasphemy against God, to blaspheme
his name, and his tabernacle, and them that dwell
in heaven. And it was given unto him to make war
with the saints, and to overcome them: and power
was given him over all kindreds, and tongues, and
nations. And all that dwell upon the earth shall
worship him, whose names are not written in the
book of life of the Lamb slain from the foundation
of the world. If any man have an ear, let him hear.*
(Revelation 13:2-9)

The definition of *antichrist* is a person or force seen as oppos-
ing Christ or the Christian Church. And while today, just as in
John's day, we have many antichrists in the world, the Bible tells
us of one man who will rise to power as an irresistible leader. He
will be *the Antichrist* – a fine speaking, delightful, persuasive,
and easy-to-like man with much military know-how who will
say he brings peace, but it will be a false peace. Even though the
Bible doesn't tell us exactly who the Antichrist is, the Scriptures
are very clear regarding his traits and characteristics, as well
as what he will do once he has the power.

In Revelation 13:3, we see that people will follow this Antichrist, and Daniel 8:23-24 tells us more about the man to whom people will be flocking: *And in the latter time of their kingdom, when the transgressors are come to the full, a king of fierce countenance, and understanding dark sentences, shall stand up. And his power shall be mighty, but not by his own power: and he shall destroy wonderfully, and shall prosper, and practise, and shall destroy the mighty and the holy people.* The *dark sentences* refer to his involvement with occult mysteries. In short, he will be filled with satanic power and will be able to do the works of Satan *with all power and signs and lying wonders* (2 Thessalonians 2:9).

Scripture also tells us where the Antichrist comes from. Unlike the true Christ, he is a Gentile who rises from the old Roman Empire. In Daniel 9:26, the Antichrist is referred to as *the prince that shall come*, and he will require people to worship him and to take the mark on their hand or forehead as his follower. Without this mark, *no man might buy or sell, save he that had the mark, or the name of the beast, or the number of his name* (Revelation 13:17).

However, God's Word warns that *if any man worship the beast and his image, and receive his mark in his forehead, or in his hand, the same shall drink of the wine of the wrath of God, which is poured out without mixture into the cup of his indignation; and he shall be tormented with fire and brimstone in the presence of the holy angels, and in the presence of the Lamb* (Revelation 14:9-10). Those who won't accept the mark of the beast will face martyrdom. *These are they which came out of great tribulation, and have washed their robes, and made them white in the blood of the Lamb* (Revelation 7:14).

The following are other Bible verses that describe the Antichrist:

And the ten horns out of this kingdom are ten kings that shall arise: and another shall rise after them; and he shall be diverse from the first, and he shall subdue three kings.

And he shall speak great words against the most High, and shall wear out the saints of the most High, and think to change times and laws: and they shall be given into his hand until a time and times and the dividing of time. (Daniel 7:24-25)

And he shall confirm the covenant with many for one week: and in the midst of the week he shall cause the sacrifice and the oblation to cease, and for the overspreading of abominations he shall make it desolate, even until the consummation, and that determined shall be poured upon the desolate. (Daniel 9:27)

Let no man deceive you by any means: for that day shall not come, except there come a falling away first, and that man of sin be revealed, the son of perdition; who opposeth and exalteth himself above all that is called God, or that is worshipped; so that he as God sitteth in the temple of God, shewing himself that he is God. (2 Thessalonians 2:3-4)

And I stood upon the sand of the sea, and saw a beast rise up out of the sea, having seven heads and ten horns, and upon his horns ten crowns, and upon his heads the name of blasphemy.

And the beast which I saw was like unto a leopard, and his feet were as the feet of a bear, and his mouth as the mouth of a lion: and the dragon gave

him his power, and his seat, and great authority.
(Revelation 13:1-2)

Return of Christ

At the end of Revelation 19, we see that Jesus comes, riding a white horse. Verse 11 says the rider's name is *Faithful and True, and in righteousness he doth judge and make war*. When he returns, the armies of heaven follow Him upon white horses, clothed in fine, white linen (verse 14). A sharp sword comes from his mouth (verse 15). A sword is an instrument that divides, and this is the judgment of the nations (verse 15). John gave us the big picture, while Jesus gave us specifics regarding this judgment in the parable of the sheep and the goats. *And before him shall be gathered all nations: and he shall separate them one from another, as a shepherd divideth his sheep from the goats* (Matthew 25:32). He separates the sheep from the goats. The sheep enter the thousand-year kingdom where Jesus reigns from Jerusalem as King. The goats are killed by the sword that comes from His mouth. When the Jews see Him, *they shall look upon me whom they have pierced, and they shall mourn for him, as one mourneth for his only son, and shall be in bitterness for him, as one that is in bitterness for his firstborn* (Zechariah 12:10). This is also the time when the Antichrist (also known as the beast) and the false prophet are thrown into the lake of fire, and Satan is bound and thrown into the bottomless pit for a thousand years.

This judgment is also depicted in Christ's parable of the wheat and the tares, showing that at the end of the tribulation all unbelievers will be judged for their sin and unbelief. They will be removed from the presence of God, while believers will reign with Him in His earthly kingdom. *Let both grow together until the harvest: and in the time of harvest I will say to the reapers,*

Gather ye together first the tares, and bind them in bundles to burn them: but gather the wheat into my barn (Matthew 13:30). The disciples did not understand this parable, so after Jesus sent the multitudes away, they asked Him to explain:

> *He answered and said unto them, He that soweth the good seed is the Son of man; the field is the world; the good seed are the children of the kingdom; but the tares are the children of the wicked one; the enemy that sowed them is the devil; the harvest is the end of the world; and the reapers are the angels.*

> *As therefore the tares are gathered and burned in the fire; so shall it be in the end of this world. The Son of man shall send forth his angels, and they shall gather out of his kingdom all things that offend, and them which do iniquity; and shall cast them into a furnace of fire: there shall be wailing and gnashing of teeth.*

> *Then shall the righteous shine forth as the sun in the kingdom of their Father.* (Matthew 13:37-43)

The Thousand-Year Reign (Messianic Kingdom)

Following the battle of Armageddon, Christ will set up His kingdom here on earth and occupy the throne of David (Acts 2:29-30). The messianic kingdom is populated by the Lord's people. In Revelation 20:4, we see them seated on thrones and judgment is given to them. *And I saw thrones, and they sat upon them, and judgment was given unto them: and I saw the souls of them that were beheaded for the witness of Jesus, and for the word of God, and which had not worshipped the beast, neither his image, neither had received his mark upon their*

*foreheads, or in their hands; and they lived and reigned with
Christ a thousand years.*

Over the thousand years, the people living in the kingdom
will still have a choice of whether or not to believe in their King.
Even though He reigns here on earth from Jerusalem, some
people will still choose to reject Him and will come against
Him at the end of the thousand years, when Satan is let out
of the pit for one last time to gather the nations against Him:

> *And when the thousand years are expired, Satan
> shall be loosed out of his prison, and shall go out to
> deceive the nations which are in the four quarters of
> the earth, Gog and Magog, to gather them together to
> battle: the number of whom is as the sand of the sea.*
>
> *And they went up on the breadth of the earth, and
> compassed the camp of the saints about, and the
> beloved city: and fire came down from God out of
> heaven, and devoured them.*
>
> *And the devil that deceived them was cast into the
> lake of fire and brimstone, where the beast and the
> false prophet are, and shall be tormented day and
> night for ever and ever.* (Revelation 20:7-10)

Satan will gather a large army and surround the city of God,
but fire will come down and consume them, and the devil
who deceived them will be thrown into the lake of fire to be
tormented forever.

Great White Throne Judgment

> *And I saw a great white throne, and him that sat
> on it. . . . And I saw the dead, small and great,
> stand before God; and the books were opened: and
> another book was opened, which is the book of life:*

*and the dead were judged out of those things which
were written in the books, according to their works.*
(Revelation 20:11-12)

The great white throne judgment is the judgment of the unbelieving dead, meaning they have not been regenerated with the
life God offered them through Jesus. Their works will mean
nothing to God, because Christ was not in them (Matthew
7:21-23). In fact, it appears that the lost will be judged based
on their evil works, and a worse damnation given to the worst.

This is the destruction of everything corrupted by sin. Even
the earth and the heaven will flee from His presence, because
at the end of this judgment, there is a new heaven and a new
earth (Revelation 20:11; 21:1).

*Then cometh the end, when he shall have deliv-
ered up the kingdom to God, even the Father; when
he shall have put down all rule and all authority
and power. For he must reign, till he hath put all
enemies under his feet. The last enemy that shall be
destroyed is death.* (1 Corinthians 15:24-26)

Judgment Seat of Christ

*For we must all appear before the judgment seat of
Christ; that every one may receive the things done in
his body, according to that he hath done, whether it
be good or bad.* (2 Corinthians 5:10)

The judgment seat of Christ is different from the great white
throne judgment. The judgment seat is for rewards, much
like we see at the Olympic games as participants are judged
on their performance and rewarded for how well they do. In
this case, only those in the body of Christ are judged. This is
the judgment of the believers' works, not to determine where
they spend eternity, but whether they receive rewards for their

works. *Good works* refer to what we do for Christ under the Holy Spirit's power. First Corinthians 3:13-15 says that our works will be shown for what they are. If what has been built withstands the test of fire, it will be rewarded:

> *Every man's work shall be made manifest: for the day shall declare it, because it shall be revealed by fire; and the fire shall try every man's work of what sort it is.*

> *If any man's work abide which he hath built thereupon, he shall receive a reward.*

> *If any man's work shall be burned, he shall suffer loss: but he himself shall be saved; yet so as by fire.*

The apostle Paul reassured the believers of their just reward when he said: *Knowing that whatsoever good thing any man doeth, the same shall he receive of the Lord, whether he be bond or free* (Ephesians 6:8). He also made this point as he was encouraging the Roman believers not to judge one another: *But why dost thou judge thy brother? Or why dost thou set at nought thy brother? For we shall all stand before the judgment seat of Christ. . . . So then every one of us shall give account of himself to God* (Romans 14:10, 12).

New Heaven and a New Earth

> *For, behold, I create new heavens and a new earth: and the former shall not be remembered, nor come into mind. (Isaiah 65:17)*

Following the great white throne judgment, God will create a new heaven and a new earth. There will be no more death, and Jesus will give up the throne to God the Father. The new Jerusalem will come down from heaven, and everything will be changed. There will no longer be day and night in the new

Jerusalem, because the Lamb is the light. *And the city had no need of the sun, neither of the moon, to shine in it: for the glory of God did lighten it, and the Lamb is the light thereof* (Revelation 21:23). *And God shall wipe away all tears from their eyes; and there shall be no more death, neither sorrow, nor crying, neither shall there be any more pain: for the former things are passed away* (Revelation 21:4). And those who enter are they who are written in the Lamb's book of life.

Further Bible passage for study: Revelation 21

Conclusion

While the end times scenario feels overwhelmingly bleak for the world, that is not the case for true believers, because those who follow the beast *make war with the Lamb, and the Lamb shall overcome them: for he is Lord of lords, and King of kings: and they that are with him are called, and chosen, and faithful* (Revelation 17:14).

As believers, we should be ready to meet our Savior. This isn't an event we should fear. As His children, the thought should elate us and fill us with hope and confidence. After all, we know the end of the story. As we wait for Him, we should have within us a deep longing to be found faithful when He returns. We should also be filled with compassion for unbelievers, because we understand the consequences.

This chapter only begins to scratch the surface regarding the information the Lord has provided us about end times. As you study further, remember that as history unfolds, we are working toward the completion of God's eternal purposes and His triumphant return as the risen Lord.

Further Bible passages for study: Matthew 25:31–46; Revelation 19:11–16.

Prayer

Our Father in heaven, Your Son has declared that He is the Alpha and Omega, the beginning and the end, the first and the last. His revelation to the apostle John gives us a clear understanding of the future. Lord, let us accept and love these commandments, for You have said, "If you love Me, keep My commandments." Lord, we love You with all our heart, soul, strength, and mind. We thank You for sharing these visions of the future so we understand the seasons ahead, understand heaven and hell, and understand the gracious love and justice You will bestow upon believers and unbelievers alike. Let us not be divided, but unified, on our understanding of the end times, so we are better prepared to respond to the times in which we live. In Jesus' name, Amen.

AFTERWORD

One Man's Story

I was led to believe that if one is born Amish, he is automatically a Christian from birth. But to continue being a Christian throughout life, I had to follow the Amish ways to the best of *my* ability. I was taught and understood the Amish ways to be a lengthy list of things to do and follow. Some of the items on the list had been passed on to us by our forefathers. Others were taken straight out of the Bible.

My Amish church believed that if one disobeyed his parents, no matter how young or how old the child is, he disobeyed God at the same time. The two went hand in hand. We were taught that parental obedience was the first and most important command on the list. We believed this because of what the apostle Paul wrote in the book of Ephesians. *Children, obey your parents in the Lord: for this is right. Honour thy father and mother; which is the **first commandment** with promise* (Ephesians 6:1-2). There was no distinction made between underage children and adult children. We were bound to obey our parents' commands until death.

If a person wanted to go to heaven at the end of his life,

he had to dress plain, be honest, work hard, get baptized to become a member of the Amish church, be separated from the non-Amish world, believe in Jesus Christ, and make a vow to follow the handwritten ordinance letter. It was a package deal. To rebel against any one of the items on the list meant that he could die and be cast into hell.

If one stood up and said he had assurance of salvation, he was boasting in self. Instead, he could only hope that God would accept him. It was all based on how well he lived the Amish way.

We considered ourselves unworthy of God and agreed that our sins were many. However, when we compared ourselves with the outside world, we immediately felt better. The outside world believed in divorce and remarriage. We didn't. They went to war with other countries. We didn't. The outside world had a government that was corrupt. They had law enforcement officers and prisons. Unmarried couples lived together, and people robbed and sometimes murdered each other. We didn't do any of those things. Instead, we helped each other out when anyone had a need. We lived uniform lives and belonged to the Anabaptist movement. Therefore, we thought we did the better biblical things. Though we believed our sins were many, we also believed that if we did our very best to measure up to our parents, the church, and God, Jesus' grace would fill in where we came up short.

Conclusion of the Story

In my story of being lost and found, I had to ask the questions: Where was I in my spiritual journey? Had I trusted in Christ by faith for the forgiveness of my sins? I had to make a choice, for there are only two. I was already on my own selfish path, but it didn't bring me any satisfaction. The only other choice was God's path – according to His Word, and not according to Amish tradition.

Jesus said, *Repent, for the kingdom of heaven is at hand* (Matthew 4:17). What did that mean? I already felt sorry for my sins, and it just made me feel more ashamed and unhappy. I learned that repentance means to change your mind about something or to change directions. I had to turn *from* the teachings I grew up with that were contrary to Scripture and turn *to* Christ's teachings in the Bible. I couldn't do this until I understood God's view of sin. I thought that much of what I was doing was okay, until I compared myself with God's law – *to him that knoweth to do good and doeth it not, to him it is sin* (James 4:17). God commands *all men every where to repent* (Acts 17:30). I was a selfish, proud, lying, lustful man in God's eyes, and I willfully chose to agree with Him and go His direction.

My next step in life was to place my faith in Jesus Christ – not just say, "Jesus Christ is the Son of God," but to believe it. Do you know what that requires? First let me say that faith only comes by hearing the Word of God (Romans 10:17). How can we come to faith if we have to read the Bible in a language we hardly understand? It is defeating the purpose. Philippians 2:10 says to bow the knee to the name of Jesus. That means a surrender of our will to do His. I not only agreed with God about my sinfulness, but I also believed that He took the guilt and shame of my sin onto Himself and died in my place on the cross. That means that I am free from the punishment of my sin – free from the wrath of God to come (Romans 5:9). Because of Christ's death, burial, and resurrection I am justified – cleared of my guilt. My so-called good works had nothing to do with it (Romans 5:1).

As a result of the shed blood of Christ, I, through repentance and faith, was born again (John 3:3, 5). My inner man was regenerated, made new! I now have a new way of seeing things – new thoughts, new words, and new actions (2 Corinthians 5:17). I am now a partaker of the divine nature (2 Peter 1:4). God has written His law of love on my heart (Hebrews 8:10). I no longer have to obey God's law because I'm required to do so. I obey Him because I want to! I love Him, because He first loved me.

> *That if thou shalt confess with thy mouth the Lord Jesus, and shalt believe in thine heart that God hath raised him from the dead, thou shalt be saved. For with the heart man believeth unto righteousness; and with the mouth confession is made unto salvation.* (Romans 10:9-10)

Prayer

Thank You, Father, for sending Your Son, Jesus Christ, to die on the cross so our sins could be forgiven. Thank You for providing the gift of eternal life and making it available to all who place their trust in Jesus Christ.

Many people on earth are living a lie. They trust in their own works for salvation, and they hardly read their Bible or talk about You to anyone. They don't fully grasp the fact that You want a real relationship with them, and that they must be born again.

Father, I don't want them to miss out on the amazingness of heaven. Please show them that You are real. Draw them to Yourself and open their blind eyes and deaf ears. Help them understand the truth about Jesus Christ and the finished work on the cross. May today be the day of salvation for many people. In Jesus' name, I pray. Amen.

AMISH POPULATION
<u>ACROSS AMERICA</u>

A s of May 2016, the estimated Amish population was 308,030. This includes both children and adults and covers thirty-one US states and three Canadian provinces. Recently, the Amish started two new settlements on Prince Edward Island, Canada.

The population number only includes horse-and-buggy Amish. Car-driving Amish, such as the Beachy Amish and Amish Mennonites, are not included.

In the fall of 2015, some New Order Amish from Ohio established settlements in Bolivia and Argentina, in South America. These smaller settlements are not included in the North American population.

Fifteen new settlements were started during the past year; eight other settlements failed.

Ohio, Pennsylvania, and Indiana continue to make up about two-thirds of the 308,030 population.

Amish families average five or more children. At least 85 percent of the population joins the Amish church. A few outsiders have joined the Amish.

The population and other 2016 statistics were taken from the *Young Center for Anabaptist and Pietist Studies, Elizabethtown College* website.

308,080 Amish People Living In The U.S. and Canada

* A New Amish Community is formed, on average, every 3-1/2 weeks.
* The Amish population may exceed 1,000,000 by 2050.
* The Amish population doubles every 20 years.

■ ....Amish
■ ....No Amish

Amish Population By State

State/Province	Settlements	Church Districts	Estimated Population
Ohio	58	537	72,495
Pennsylvania	55	479	70,890
Indiana	22	369	51,660
New York	51	136	18,360
Wisconsin	51	141	18,050
Michigan	45	109	14,495
Missouri	43	98	11,465
Kentucky	41	83	10,375
Iowa	23	63	9,070
Illinois	19	55	7,095
Ontario	16	40	5,400
Minnesota	21	36	4,535
Tennessee	9	22	2,750
Kansas	7	15	2,025
Delaware	1	10	1,500
Maryland	3	11	1,485
Virginia	6	8	1,080
Oklahoma	4	7	945
Maine	5	6	810
Nebraska	4	5	675
Colorado	4	5	675
Montana	4	5	675
West Virginia	3	3	405
Arkansas	2	2	270
North Carolina	2	2	170
Mississippi	1	2	150
Florida	1	2	150
South Dakota	1	1	75
Idaho	1	1	75
Texas	1	1	75
Wyoming	1	1	75
Texas	1	1	75
Prince Edward Island	2	2	30
New Brunswick	1	1	25
Vermont	1	1	20
Total	509	2,259	308,030

FREE CORRESPONDENCE
BIBLE STUDY COURSES

Simply check the box by the course you want, fill out the other side of this form, and mail it back to us. We will then send you the first lesson in the course that you requested. Choose one of our current courses:

☐ **Bible Basics:** What does the Bible say about forgiveness of sins and being born again? (1 lesson)

☐ **Life's Struggles:** Find biblical wisdom for overcoming fear, pride, doubt, anger, and worry. (3 lessons)

☐ **Book of Books:** Consider the history, customs, geography, and measurements of biblical times. See how the Old and New Testaments fit together. Learn how God's Word applies to your life today. (13 lessons)

☐ **Foundational Study:** Study what the Bible says about foundational topics like the new birth, forgiveness, friends, prayer, everlasting life, brokenness, wisdom, lying, salvation, judgment, the Christian home, victory, and getting your life back on track. (3 lessons)

☐ **Verse-by-Verse Study:** Travel verse by verse through parts or all of the biblical books of John, Ephesians, Colossians, 1 John, Titus, and Luke. (9 lessons)

☐ **Topical Study:** Study what the Bible says about topics like how to pray, the Bible is the Word of God, faith, fighting loneliness, doubt and disbelief, fighting temptation, hatred, and more. (12 lessons)

Name _____

Mailing Address _____

City _____ St. _____ Zip _____

Date of Birth _____

Make sure you checked the box by the course you want, and include the page showing the courses, as well as this page with your address.

Mail this page to:
Plowman's Academy
PO Box 128
Savannah, OH 44874

If you have any other questions or thoughts regarding what you read in this book, please contact MAP Ministry at the same address, or call 419-962-1515.

Cut here

Other Similar Titles

By MAP Ministry
And Aneko Press

This booklet contains the Gospel of John in three languages: German, PA Dutch and KJV. In addition to the Gospel of John being printed in three languages – side by side – there's a fourth column that shares easy to understand commentary notes from three people; one from an English background, one from an Old Order Amish background and one from an Old Order Mennonite background.

Available from MAP Ministry

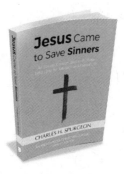

This is a heart-level conversation with you, the reader. Every excuse, reason, and roadblock for not coming to Christ is examined and duly dealt with. If you think you may be too bad, or if perhaps you really are bad and you sin either openly or behind closed doors, you will discover that life in Christ is for you too. You can reject the message of salvation by faith, or you can choose to live a life of sin after professing faith in Christ, but you cannot change the truth as it is, either for yourself or for others. As such, it behooves you and your family to embrace truth, claim it for your own, and be genuinely set free for now and eternity. Come, and embrace this free gift of God, and live a victorious life for Him.

Available FREE from MAP Ministry